ARCHITECTURAL
WONDERS

Published by
Kandour Limited
Monticello House
45 Russell Square
London WC1B 4JP
United Kingdom

First published 2007

10 9 8 7 6 5 4 3 2 1

Managing Editor: Ruth Urbom

Project Editor: Christina Czapiewska

Editorial Assistant: Emma Agyemang

Creative Director: Alexander Rose

Jacket Design: Alex Ingr

Design Layout: Daniel Oliver

Art Editor: David Fraser

Production Manager: Carol Titchener

Sales & Editorial Manager: Karen Lomax

Authors: Jessica Renison and Jody Thompson

Additional Material: Kaspa Hazlewood and Wendy Johnson

Text Copyright © Kandour Limited 2007

Design Copyright © Kandour Limited 2007

Printed and bound in Singapore

ISBN 13: 978-1-905741-65-6

A catalogue record of this book is available from the British Library

ARCHITECTURAL WONDERS

THE WORLD'S GREATEST BUILDINGS

JESSICA RENISON AND JODY THOMPSON

Kandour Ltd

Contents

Inset: Architectural contrasts in the heart of Manhattan.

Right: The Empire State Building towers over the city below.

Empire State Building

The Empire State Building was an early contender in the "race to the sky" that emerged from the burgeoning wealth of the 1920s and '30s and epitomized the flamboyant and feel-good Jazz Age.

The Empire State Building is a 102-story Art Deco structure that scrapes the sky a quarter of a mile (402 m) above street level. Art Deco was the first architectural style in the United States to break away from the "revivalist" tradition. Up to that time, Greek Revival and Gothic Revival were the norms for grand civic structures, but Art Deco was all about the future. In simple terms, it could be described as an attempt to transfer the sleekness associated with the Machine Age into art, architecture, and design in general. Art Deco in buildings was a symbolic expression of the technological invention exploding across the developed world. One classic Art Deco feature, however, is in fact accidental rather than designed. The tiered structure which is typically Art Deco, and which some say shows an Egyptian influence following the discovery in 1920 of Tutankhamen's tomb, was in fact dictated by necessity. The tall, rectangular skyscrapers were blocking light to sidewalks, so it was decreed that upper stories be "stepped back" to allow more light to reach through. As a result, the tapering building became a feature of Art Deco.

The Empire State Building was an early contender in the "race to the sky" that

emerged from the burgeoning wealth of the 1920s and '30s—the flamboyant and feel-good Jazz Age. In a series of events that foreshadowed the Space Race of the 1960s, the capitalist giants of the United States began a race to build the tallest building in the world. It is sometimes claimed that the initial impetus came from Paris' Eiffel Tower of 1889, which America saw as an unspoken challenge. Ironically, a committee of artists set up to oppose the building of the Eiffel Tower on the grounds that it was "grotesque" and "mercantile," claimed in a sideways snipe: "even the commercial Americans would not want this Eiffel Tower." Whilst Walter Chrysler of the Chrysler Corporation was busy constructing his building, the former vice president of General Motors, John Jacob Raskob, entered the race to build the modern day Tower of Babel. He bought the land on which the Waldorf-Astoria hotel had sat, and which the success of Grand Central Station had made a prime location in an increasingly prosperous area. Raskob paid $16 million for the land, and promptly hired the firm of architects Shreve, Lamb, and Harmon to design the building that would win the race to the sky. His design brief was simple: "How high can you build so

that it won't fall down?" William Lamb soon presented him with an equally simple solution: "A certain amount of space in the center, arranged as compactly as possible, contains the vertical circulation, mail chutes, toilets, shafts, and corridors. Surrounding this is a perimeter of office space 28 feet (8.5 m) deep. The sizes of the floors diminish as the elevators decrease in number. In essence there is a pyramid of non-rentable space surrounded by a greater pyramid of rentable space."

When Raskob saw the final designs for the building, his desperation to win the race prompted him to comment: "It needs a hat." That "hat" was to be the airship mast that tops the 102nd story. In the 1930s, airships—or "dirigibles" as they were known—were thought to be the future for an air-traveling generation. What could be a more fitting accessory for the Art Deco building to beat all other buildings? The age of airship travel was soon over, however, and even at the time was heading swiftly towards its humble fate as an advertising billboard. Besides which, the few attempts made at mooring ships on the mast were undeniably hazardous, and the Art Deco spire soon went out of service. The Empire State Building and the

Over: The Empire State Building towers above New York City's jostling skyscrapers. The spire was originally intended as a mast for airships, but was hardly ever used as such.

and involved 3,400 laborers, largely European immigrants and Mohawk nation iron workers. It consists of a frame constructed out of 60,000 tons of Pittsburgh steel, which is coated in Indiana limestone and granite. Initially, its full height measured 1,250 feet (381 m), but in the 1950s, a television antenna was added which brought it up to 1,453 feet (443 m).

But what began as an Art Deco monument to America's private wealth suddenly hit the rocks of the Great Depression. The capitalist race had been won by Raskob, but it ground to a sudden and immediate halt. The building's first years were blighted by financial loss, as unrented office space caused the venture to leak money very quickly. The building was to be dubbed "The Empty State Building." However, what it lost in office rental in the early days, it has since more than made up for in income from tourism. The Empire State Building is one of the most visited tourist attractions in the world. The observation deck on the 86th floor, with its stunning 360-degree view of the city, has become known as a romantic spot—made famous by movies such as *An Affair to Remember* and *Sleepless in Seattle*. And of course its place in movie history was secured when King Kong, with struggling heroine in hand, scaled its lofty heights. The building has also known its fair share of disaster, however, most notably in 1945 when a B-25 Mitchell bomber caught in thick fog crashed into the north side between the 79th and 80th floors, killing 14 people.

Above: The jagged landscape of New York City, with the Hudson River in the background. The peak of the Empire State Building is visible all over the city.

Opposite: An advanced lighting system is used to express support, from rooting for the local teams, to extending an arm of comfort and solidarity in the wake of the 9/11 attacks.

Chrysler Building were neck and neck, and neither party would reveal how high it was going. A member of the Empire State party later recalled: "We thought we would be the tallest at 80 stories. Then the Chrysler went higher, so we lifted the Empire State to 85 stories. Raskob was worried that Walter Chrysler would pull a trick—like hiding a rod in the spire and then sticking it up at the last minute." In the event, Raskob beat Chrysler, and the Empire State building,—which echoes the nickname of New York State—stood as the tallest building in the world, and it continued to for more than 40 years. Completed in 1931, it took only one year to build

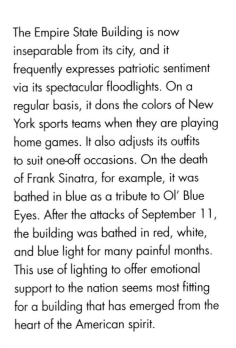

The Empire State Building is now inseparable from its city, and it frequently expresses patriotic sentiment via its spectacular floodlights. On a regular basis, it dons the colors of New York sports teams when they are playing home games. It also adjusts its outfits to suit one-off occasions. On the death of Frank Sinatra, for example, it was bathed in blue as a tribute to Ol' Blue Eyes. After the attacks of September 11, the building was bathed in red, white, and blue light for many painful months. This use of lighting to offer emotional support to the nation seems most fitting for a building that has emerged from the heart of the American spirit.

Above: The observation deck on the 86th floor provides a 360-degree view of the city.

Over: The Empire State Building won the race to the sky in 1931, but was subsequently beaten by the twin towers of the World Trade Center.

Right: The Australian flag flying proudly against a clear blue sky from the crest of Sydney Harbor Bridge.

Sydney Harbor Bridge

The majestic Sydney Harbor Bridge, known affectionately to locals as "The Coat Hanger," is the world's largest steel arch bridge and spans one of the most beautiful natural harbors on the planet.

As the world's largest steel arch bridge, spanning one of the most beautiful natural harbors on the planet, the majestic structure of the Sydney Harbor Bridge has become an international symbol of Australia.

Known affectionately by locals as "The Coat Hanger" because of its curved appearance, it might not be the longest steel arch bridge—that honor belongs to the bridge crossing the New River Gorge in the USA—but it is the world's largest. And its vital statistics are impressive.

Its total length is 3,770 feet (1149 m) and its arch span is 1,650 feet (503 m). The top of the arch is 440 feet (134 m) above sea level, though that can increase by as much as 7 inches (180 mm) in the hot Sydney sun as a result of the steel expanding in the heat. Two large metal hinges at the base of the bridge accommodate these expansions and contractions and thereby prevent the arch from being damaged. The total steelwork weighs 52,800 tons, including 39,000 tons in the arch, and it carries eight vehicle lanes, two train lines, a pedestrian lane, and a bike lane. Originally, there were two tram tracks, but these were replaced by two of the road lanes in 1958.

Sydney Harbor Bridge provides a dramatic vista as it crosses the harbor at its narrowest point between Dawes and Milsons Point at Port Jackson, providing a link between the city's central business district and the north shore. It is held together with six million rivets, with a reinforced concrete deck and reinforced concrete pylons. When it was officially opened in March 1932, it was considered the pinnacle of bridge design and engineering invention.

Although suggestions to build a bridge across the harbor had been afoot since 1815, the genesis of the current bridge started in 1890, when a royal commission decided that a bridge was needed to relieve the heavy level of ferry traffic in the harbor.

Up until the end of the nineteenth century, many bridges in Australia had been constructed of timber, with more expensive, heavy cast iron and masonry used for only a few structures meant to carry larger volumes of traffic. It was only with the advent of the twentieth century and the advances in technology, with reinforced concrete and prefabricated steel components making large-scale bridge projects more feasible.

Above: A heart illuminating this much-loved Australian landmark at night.

As time went on, passenger ferry services in Sydney Harbor quickly reached a critical point. Delays and accidents due to congestion were increasing. The only other way to travel between the "two Sydneys" on either side of the harbor was to take a 30-mile (50 km) trip around the perimeter. In order to boost the local economy and promote development of Sydney's North Shore, a major bridge across the harbor was clearly necessary. Designs and proposals were requested in 1900, but it wasn't until 1912 that John Bradfield was appointed chief engineer of the project. After traveling across the world to look at other bridges, he decided to base his idea on New York's Hell Gate Bridge and finished his formal design in 1916. However, building was delayed until 1922 because of World War I.

In November 1922 the New South Wales (NSW) parliament passed laws that finally gave the go-ahead for the bridge's construction, and the tender was won by a British company, Dorman, Long and Co. Ltd. Bradfield promised that, despite this foreign involvement, the majority of the workforce building the bridge would be Australian.

Right: A classic nighttime view of Sydney Harbor Bridge with the Opera House in the foreground.

However, the relationship between the British builders and Bradfield did not remain cordial for long. When Sir Ralph Freeman was hired by Dorman, Long and Co Ltd. to refine the finished design in further detail, a bitter disagreement broke out between Bradfield and Freeman as to who actually designed the bridge.

The bridge took eight years to build, starting in 1925. Over 2,000 people were involved in the day-to-day construction work, including engineers, boilermakers, ironworkers, and stonemasons. Although most were indeed Australian, some skilled laborers, such as stonemasons and ironworkers, were brought from overseas.

It was no easy place to work, either. Sixteen men died while building the bridge, mostly by falling off the bridge, and accidents on the job were frequent as it was in the days before health and safety laws. The rivet cooker's job, for example, involved throwing red-hot rivets to the rivet catchers, who caught them in buckets and then hammered them into place. Certainly not an occupation for the fainthearted—especially when hanging hundreds of feet above land and sea in the process! However, as the bridge was constructed during the Depression, any job was welcome, and the bridge earned the nickname "The Iron Lung" as a result.

The steel used for the bridge was largely imported. About 79 percent came from Middlesbrough in the Northeast of England, with the rest

made in Australia. The granite used was quarried in Moruya, New South Wales, and the concrete used was also Australian-made. The rivets, meanwhile, were manufactured in Lancashire, England.

In September 1930, the arch was joined in the middle, and work began to lay the road deck and to build the pylons that anchor the bridge at either end. By February 1932, the bridge was completed and its weight bearing was tested by laying 96 locomotive engines end-to-end along the railway tracks the length of the bridge.

The two pairs of pylons at each end are about 276 feet (89 m) high and are made of concrete and granite, while the abutments, which support the ends of the bridge, are buried in the base of each structure. Other than that, the pylons serve no structural purpose and are primarily to visually balance the bridge itself. The pylons are used variously now as a museum, tourist center, and a lookout for the harbor.

The official opening ceremony for the bridge was not without controversy. It was set to take place on March 19, 1932, with the then Premier of NSW, Labor politician Jack Lang, to cut a ribbon at its southern end and declare it open.

However, just as Lang stepped forward with the scissors before the millions of people watching, a man in military uniform galloped forward on horseback and slashed the ribbon with a sword, declaring the bridge to be open "in

the name of His Majesty the King and the decent and respectable citizens of New South Wales." He was promptly arrested. The ribbon was hurriedly retied and Lang performed the official opening ceremony. After he did so, there was a 21-gun salute and a Royal Australian Air Force flyby.

The man on horseback, Francis de Groot, was convicted of offensive behavior and was fined £5. He was a member of a right-wing paramilitary group called the New Guard, which was opposed to Lang's leftist policies.

Once the bridge had opened to traffic, it cost a horse and rider three pence and a car six pence to cross. Now horses and riders are no longer allowed to cross, but you can bicycle across in a special lane and walk across the bridge for free. Cars cost around $2.70 ($AU 3.30) for a southbound trip and it is free to go northbound.

To celebrate the 75th anniversary of the opening of the Sydney Harbor Bridge, over 200,000 people walked across the bridge (which was closed to other traffic for the day) as part of the Our Bridge Celebrations in March 2007. The festivities were officially opened by dignitaries including the Governor and Premier of New South Wales.

Rumor has it that the large numbers of schoolchildren who walked across the bridge as part of the opening ceremony in 1932 were warned not to march in step, in case the bridge collapsed under

their rhythmic footsteps! The 75th-anniversary walkers did not receive such a warning, as the bridge's sturdy construction had proven itself to be up to the task.

In 1932, the average annual daily traffic was around 11,000 and is now around 160,000 vehicles per day—despite the fact that the Sydney Harbor Tunnel was opened in 1992 to cope with increasing traffic problems in the area. That alone carries around 75,000 vehicles a day.

The total cost of the bridge was $19,850,000 ($AU 24,340,000)—double the original quote. This was not paid off in full until 1988 and maintenance costs never stop either. Every time the bridge needs a wash and brush up, it takes 570,611 pints of paint (270,000 l) to give it one coat. One of Australia's best-known celebrities Paul "Crocodile Dundee" Hogan was once one of the painters contracted for the job.

For those not satisfied with simply observing this magnificent bridge from the shore or walking across it, it is now possible to climb the bridge. Since 1998, BridgeClimb has made it possible for tourists to climb the southern half of the bridge's great arch. Tours run throughout the day, from dawn to dusk, and are only cancelled due to electrical storms or high winds. During the climb, those scaling the steel arch are secured to the bridge by a wire lifeline. At the summit, climbers cross to the western side of the arch for the descent—each climb takes three and a half hours. A challenge not for

the faint-hearted, it nevertheless attracts thousands of people every year and is open to anyone over 12 who is in good enough shape to handle some steep ascents on metal ladders and can cope with heights.

Once at the summit however, with the great sweep of Sydney Harbor, the Opera House and the other visual delights of the city before you, the climb is always worth it—especially when you realize you're on top of one the architectural wonders of the world.

Left: An Australian naval vessel cruises with ease underneath Sydney Harbor Bridge due to its immense height.

Over: Another stunning view of Sydney Harbor Bridge with the Opera House bathed in light behind it.

Golden Gate Bridge

Inset: The striking color and Art Deco details make the bridge distinguished and distinctive, both close up and from afar.

Golden Gate Bridge

Mighty and graceful, the stylized geometry of the Golden Gate Bridge makes it an elegant sculpture as much as a roadway.

"No one can bridge the Golden Gate because of the insurmountable difficulties which are apparent to all who give thought to the idea," they said. But one man proved them wrong, overcoming those "insurmountable" difficulties to create an awe-inspiring feat of engineering. Joseph Strauss dreamt of building "the biggest thing of its kind that a man could build," and because of his tenacity, that "biggest thing" stands today as one of the most powerful, most graceful structures in the world.

The magnificent, sweeping suspension bridge that crosses the Golden Gate—the juncture between the Pacific Ocean and San Francisco Bay—was the largest of its kind when it was constructed in 1937. This bay could at one time only be crossed by ferry, but today the Golden Gate Bridge forms a section of the main highway that runs along the West Coast of America. As the only exit north out of San Francisco, it is crossed daily by around 100,000 vehicles.

The original plans for the Golden Gate Bridge were the work of engineer Strauss, who up to that point was more familiar with drawbridges,

but who subsequently poured his life and soul into the project. He carefully adjusted his designs and relentlessly campaigned for funding over a period of ten years, using all means available to him—including bribery—to get his bridge built. However, the architect Irving Morrow is perhaps equally responsible for the striking impact created by the bridge, since he decided on the burnt orange color and the Art Deco details that make it such an iconic image.

Morrow, and his wife Gertrude, worked together on such details as the pedestrian railings, which they honed and simplified, the lean, angled lampposts, and the distinctive wide, vertical ribbing on the towers, which catches the sunlight as it falls on the bay. The color, known as International Orange, was chosen because it is sympathetic to the natural surroundings, allowing the bridge to fit harmoniously into the multicolored patchwork of sky, water, and land, whilst at the same time being clearly visible in the infamous coastal fogs that haunt San Francisco. Morrow had been in love with the Golden Gate long before he became involved in the project to build it. Previously an architect of small

Above: Wind-surfers are dwarfed by the Golden Gate Bridge.

Over: Irving Morrow was responsible for aesthetic details such as the lighting and the vertical stripes on the horizontal cross bars of the towers.

residential buildings, he had often admired it on his daily commute on the ferry, writing poetically, "it is loveliest at the cool end of the day when, for a few breathless moments, faint afterglows transfigure the gray line of hills." After collaborating on the Golden Gate Bridge, Morrow went back to designing small residential buildings. The bridge was the only public monument to benefit from his artistry.

Some of the geometric features typical of Art Deco design also fulfill

important functions, rather than just being decorative: for example, the graceful curves of the upper cables are hyperbola, or conic sections from geometry. The rectangular openings in the towers decrease in size with height, which has the effect of emphasizing the height of the towers.

Construction on the bridge began in 1933. It was to last nearly five years and cost $35 million. Unusually for such a construction project, a safety net was erected beneath the bridge

in an attempt to prevent fatalities. Nonetheless, 11 men died during construction, most of them at the end of the project when the net had weakened. But a further 19 had their falls broken by the net and their lives saved—later forming their own "Halfway to Hell" club. The bridge is supported by thick cables attached to two towers, each of which is planted firmly in the solid rock at either side of the bay. The towers are 746 feet (227 m) high and the distance between them measures 4,200 feet

Below: Beauty and practicality meet in an awesome feat of engineering.

Left: The supporting steel cables of this suspension bridge are 36.5 inches wide.

(1,280 m). The cables that hold the floor of the bridge are a massive 36.5 inches (92.7 cm) in diameter, every half-inch crucially necessary in supporting its length and weight. The fiendishly-difficult mathematical calculations involved allow the bridge to swing a maximum of 27 feet (8.2 m) in the highly unlikely event that a broadside wind came in off the Pacific Ocean at a speed of 100 miles an hour (160 km/h). This was considered to be the worst possible case scenario. In extremely windy conditions, the bridge closes, but this has only occurred five times in its lifetime. In 1982, the wind was so strong that the bridge could clearly be seen to roll like the sea.

There was a great deal of opposition to the building of the bridge. Amongst detractors were members of The Sierra Club, who objected on aesthetic and environmental grounds, claiming that the natural beauty of the Golden Gate

would be disturbed by what they termed "an upside down rat-trap." They counted among their members the renowned photographer and San Francisco resident Ansel Adams, who took a wistful photograph of the Golden Gate on the eve of the bridge's construction. However, Joseph Strauss held fast to his poetic vision despite the jeers all around him, and the insistence that the gap was too wide to be spanned by the bridge he envisioned. He only lived one year after its completion, but at least he saw his dreams become reality. At the end of an often discouraging, but ultimately triumphant, journey, he wrote an ode to the work entitled "The Mighty Task is Done."

An inscription on the site of the bridge bears its own testimony to his dedication:

"Here at the Golden Gate is the
Eternal Rainbow that he conceived
And set to form, a promise indeed
That the race of man shall
Endure unto the Ages."

It is possible to walk or bicycle across the Golden Gate Bridge during daylight hours, but pedestrians and cyclists must cope with strong winds that gust across the bridge. Perhaps a better way to take in the splendor of the Golden Gate Bridge is to observe its beauty in its entirety from another of San Francisco's notable locations such as Alcatraz or the Marin Headlands.

It was said at the time of its inception—as it often is—that the bridge couldn't be built, that is was an impossibility. When it finally opened, then, on May 27, 1937, it was with feelings of triumph and elation that crowds of San Franciscans thronged to walk across it. Ever since that day, it has held pride of place in the heart of the city. The finished creation, the Golden Gate Bridge, is an elegant structure, both mighty and graceful. The stylized geometry, typical of Art Deco design, makes it a sculpture as much as a roadway. During the day, the vertical fluting throws dramatic, forever changing, shadows, and at night, its sharp, slightly curved lines are highlighted by hundreds of tiny lights, giving it a touch of splendor and magic.

Left: The color International Orange was chosen because it blended well with the rich and varied colors of nature that surround the bridge.

Below: The bridge at night, still making its majestic presence felt.

Over: One of San Francisco's famous impenetrable fogs.

Petronas Twin Towers

Built in 1998, the Petronas Twin Towers were the world's tallest high-rise buildings created in the 20th century as well as the tallest twin towers in the world. Influenced by Islamic art, the Petronas Twin Towers reflect Islam, the main religion of Malaysia.

Above: Detail of the polygonal geometric design.

The Petronas Twin Towers were built in 1998 making them the world's tallest high-rise buildings created in the 20th century as well as the tallest twin towers in the world. Petronas, Petroleum Nasional Berhad, is the Malaysian national government entity responsible for all of Malaysia's oil and gas resource development. Cesar Pelli was commissioned to create the super-tall structure. Pelli is a world-renowned architectural designer known for his many skyscrapers. Having studied architecture at the Universidad Nacional de Tucuman, in Argentina, Pelli immigrated to the United States in 1952 where he finished his studies at the University of Illinois at Urbana-Champaign. He became a naturalized U.S. citizen in 1964. In the early years of his architectural career, Pelli worked with world-renowned architect Eero Sanrinen, whose firm was located in New Haven, Connecticut. Pelli eventually became known for his extensive use of curved facades and the metallic elements in his designs. In 1977, he was appointed Dean of the School of Architecture at Yale University where he served until 1984. He currently has his architectural firm in New Haven, Connecticut and employs about 100 architects. One of his most noteworthy designs is that of the World Financial Center complex in New York City. The World Financial Center complexes are the surrounding buildings to the tragically destroyed World Trade Center.

Originally, two different construction companies were hired to construct the twin towers in competition with each other. An innovative design using super high strength reinforced concrete was used in construction motivated by a lack of steel and the crippling cost of importing steel. Many Asian contractors have used high-strength concrete because they have discovered it to be twice as effective as steel construction in sway reduction. It does, however, make the building twice as heavy on its foundation compared to the foundational weight of a steel building. The towers are supported by 247-square-foot (23 m^2) concrete cores and an outer ring of widely-spaced super columns. The design provides 14,000–21,000 square feet (1300–2000 m^2) of column-free office space on each floor. The joint venture between Samsung Engineering

Left: The towers lit up at night with sky bridge visible.

Over: The Petronas Towers create a dazzling spectacle at night, rising above the vibrant city of Kuala Lumpur.

and Construction, a local firm, and Kukdong Engineering and Construction, won the race to complete Tower Two despite starting construction a month behind Tower One. The delay was due to their discovery that the structure was just under 1 inch (25 mm) off from the vertical. Hazama Corporation of Japan and J.A. Jones of the United States built Tower One.

Construction of the Twin Towers was planned on the site of the former Selangor Turf Club, but was moved when soil showed that irregularities in the limestone bedrock—known as Kenny Hill soil—would prove unsuitable. Soil tests also showed that the bedrock under both towers began shallow at 49 feet (15 m) then sharply sloped to more than 590 feet (180 m). Calculated to weigh 330,700 tons (300,000 metric tons), each tower would be spread over a concrete slab known as a mat. It was calculated that the tower weight exerted a pressure of nearly 12 tons/square foot (1,140 kilopascals), which would exceed the weight-bearing capacity of the soil. It would be enough weight to cause foundational failure. A depth of 69 feet (21 m), the equivalent of five

Petronas Towers

Right: Echoes of the Art Deco movement, as well as a strong Islamic influence, are present in the design.

Over: With a staggering 88 floors, the towers require a complex double-decker elevator system to provide efficient transportation within the building.

stories, was excavated for the basement in order to support the immense weight of the structures. At this location it would mean penetrating the bedrock at one end. Using concrete-filled piers at the deep end of the location would not only prove to be expensive and slow, but over time, the piers would shorten causing the towers to tilt. It was decided to move the construction location 197 feet (60 m) to the southeast of the initial site. The bedrock was deeper allowing the buildings to be firmly anchored in a minimum of 180 feet (55 m) of soil for each tower basement. Friction piles were used in construction reinforced by a grout mixture of sand and cement. Beginning in 1993 it took an entire year for the foundation construction phase to be completed.

On the 41st and 42nd floors, a 190-foot (58 m) skywalk spans the two towers. Suspended 558 feet (170 m) up, the skywalk is built to rotate with high winds at the top of the twin towers. Visitors must change elevators at this level to go to higher levels. Open to all visitors, except on Mondays, the skywalk can be accessed with a visitor's pass. Issued on a first-come, first-served basis, passes are free and are limited to 1400 per day— but they usually run out before noon!

The Petronas Towers held the record for being the world's tallest buildings from completion in 1998 until 2004, when the Taipei 101 super-tall skyscraper took the record. Petronas Towers has 88 floors, while the Taipei 101 has 101 floors. The Sears Tower still holds the record for having higher occupied

floors, a higher pinnacle, and a higher roof. The Taipei 101 has the greatest structural height. Due to the idiosyncrasies of the rules governing building measurements there is much controversy over the Taipei 101's claim to the title of world's tallest building. The question of counting spires but not antennas is still being debated. The Petronas Twin Towers is 1,483 feet (452 m) tall at its antenna/spire. The roof lies at 1,322 feet (403 m) and the top floor at 1,230 feet (375 m). The 88 floors give the towers a total of 4.25 million square feet. There are 78 elevators. Designed to minimize floor space, the elevators maximize the number of people they can transport. Located in the center of each tower, the main elevators are double-decker, with the lower deck carrying passengers to the odd-numbered floors and the upper deck carrying passengers to the even-numbered floors. Use of an escalator is required in order to access the upper deck of the elevator, enabling passengers to access the even-numbered floors from ground level.

In the event of an emergency evacuation of the building, passengers may walk between elevator cars. The shuttle elevator may also be used. There are only doors at levels G/1 and levels 41/42 for use in the event of fire in the lower half of the building. The enclosed shaft should remain unaffected.

Essential for Petronas Towers is the service building located to the east of the towers. The service building dissipates the heat from the air-conditioning system for all the levels in both towers.

The Petronas Company and a number of its subsidiaries and associate companies occupy all of Tower One. Tower Two is leased to other companies.

Influenced by Islamic art, the Petronas Twin Towers reflect Islam, the main religion of Malaysia. Using 32.2 square miles (83.5 sq km) of stainless steel extrusions and 21.2 square miles (55 sq km) of laminated glass to clad the twin towers, the design vision of architect Cesar Pelli was realized. It created a "multi-faceted diamond sparkling in the sun." The curtain wall exterior consists of 33,000 panels, each the height of one floor, spanning from ledge to ledge. Horizontal "bullnoses" and the "teardrop" sunscreen brackets provide shade for the building. Both features give the towers the appearance of a flowing silver ribbon surrounding the building. The laminated glass was used because it screens out most of the ultra-violet rays and for its safety, sound insulation, durability, and solar energy control. The pinnacles are clad entirely in brushed stainless steel giving it a high sheen. Light reflecting off the pinnacle gives the illusion of greater height.

"According to Lao Tse, the reality of a hollow object is in the void and not in the walls that define it. He was speaking, of course, of spiritual realities. These are the realities of the Petronas Towers. The power of the void is increased and made more explicit by the pedestrian bridge that…with its supporting structure creates a portal to the sky…a door to the infinite."
—Cesar Pelli, architect (1995)

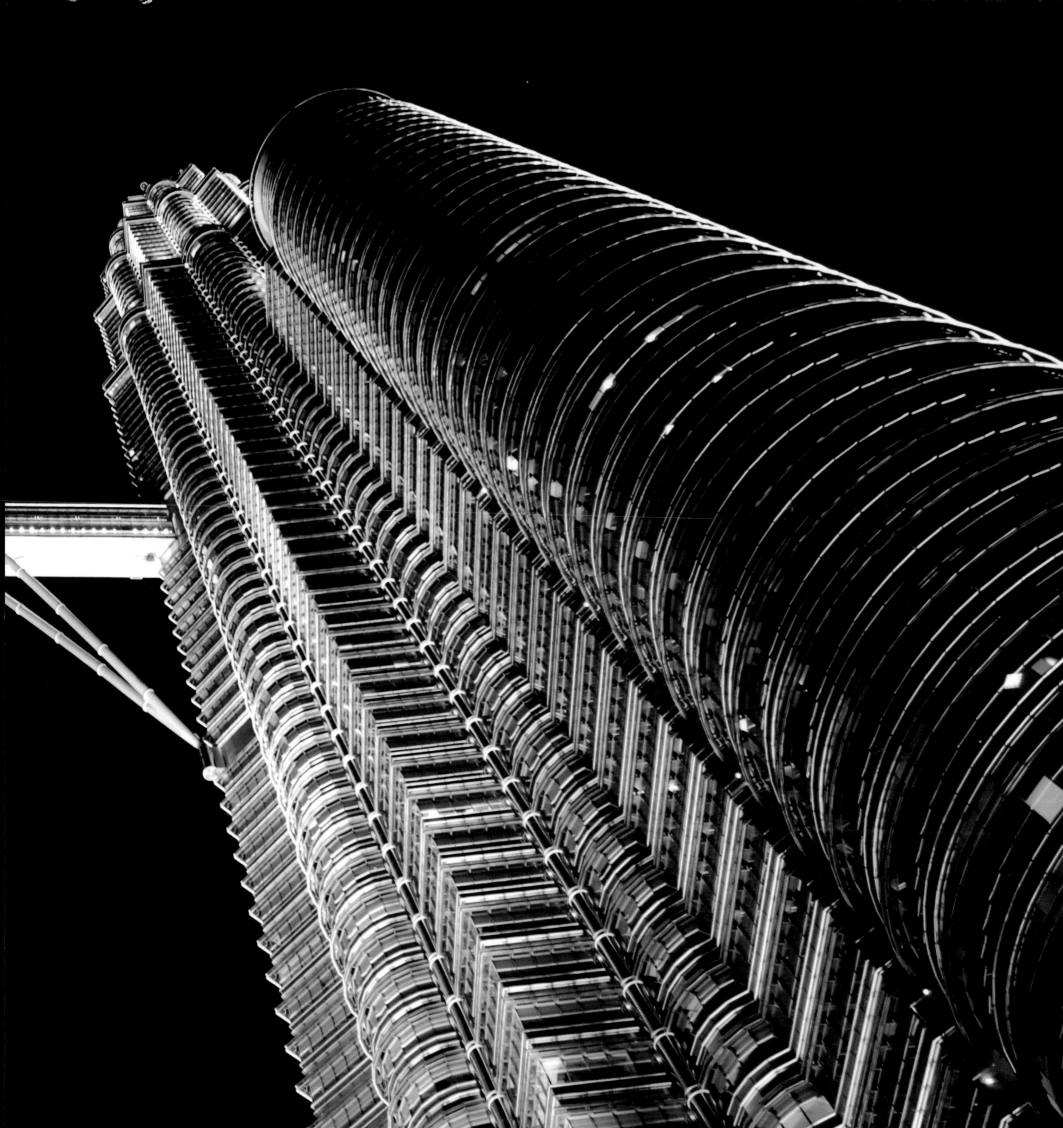

The vast concrete swathes of the Hoover Dam looking down toward the Colorado River, above, and across to the top of the structure, right.

Hoover Dam

The Hoover Dam is the highest concrete dam in the Western hemisphere. With its elegant Art Deco style, beautiful sculptures, and carved towers rising seamlessly from the dam face, the Hoover Dam attracts up to 10 million visitors each year.

One of the modern wonders of the world, Hoover Dam is the highest concrete dam in the Western hemisphere. The world's tallest dam, at 1099 feet (335 m), is Rogun Dam in Tajikistan. Built in the Black Canyon of the Colorado River, on the Arizona-Nevada border, Hoover Dam is a "gravity dam," meaning that the foundations rely on gravity to stop the structure from falling down.

Named after President Herbert Hoover—himself an engineer—the dam was also called Boulder Dam or Boulder Canyon Dam. Hoover played a central role in the construction of the dam, first as Secretary of Commerce and later as President.

The dam is used for myriad functions including flood and silt control, electric power, irrigation, and domestic and industrial water supplies. At the time of its construction, it was the largest civil engineering project in the US and cost $49 million—or $676 million in today's money.

Hoover Dam was designated a National Historic Landmark in 1985,

and, in September 2001, the American Society of Civil Engineers named it a Civil Engineering Monument of the Millennium. Completed in 1936, after five years of construction, the dam is without a doubt an incredible feat of engineering.

Standing 726 feet (221 m) high, 1,200 feet (365 m) wide across the crest, and 660 feet (201 m) thick at its base, Hoover Dam placed huge logistical requirements on its builders. They had 3.7 million cubic yards (2.8 million m³) of rock to excavate, 45 million pounds (20 million kg) of pipe and structural steel to erect, and 4.4 million cubic yards (3.4 million m³) of concrete to pour. Remarkably, the entire project was completed under budget and two years ahead of schedule.

Not only that, but it is also a structure of great beauty. With its elegant Art Deco style, beautiful sculptures, and carved towers rising seamlessly from the dam face, Hoover Dam attracts up to 10 million visitors each year.

Before the construction of the dam, the Colorado River, one of the

Above: One of the two drum-gate controlled spillways on either side of the canyon.

Over: The might of the magnificent Lake Mead behind the Hoover Dam.

Above: Some of the vast turbines housed inside the Hoover Dam, which generate a billion kilowatt-hours a year of hydroelectric power.

Opposite: The dam crosses the border between the Pacific and Mountain time zones.

most powerful rivers in the world, occasionally overflowed, causing problems for the farming communities in the river basin. A dam could therefore help control the floods, and this was its initial purpose. However, everyone soon realized that it could do a lot more—like help to irrigate the very same arid farming land.

First though, decisions had to be made on how the water should be distributed once the dam was built. The Colorado Basin states—Arizona, California, Colorado, Nevada, New Mexico, Utah, and Wyoming—all had an interest in the resources provided

by the river. There was concern, among some, that California, which was experiencing a population surge, might secure the lion's share and deprive more rural states of theirs.

As a result, a commission was formed in 1922 with a representative from each of the Basin states and an official from the government—Herbert Hoover. Then Secretary of Commerce, Hoover met with the state governors of the Basin states in January 1922 to work out how to divide the Colorado River waters fairly. Eight months later, on November 24, the Colorado River Compact was signed in Santa Fe,

New Mexico. Splitting the river basin into upper and lower halves, with the states within each half deciding how the water would be divided, the agreement was vital for the Boulder Dam Project to get off the ground.

After much legal to-ing and fro-ing between the House and the Senate, in December 1928, President Calvin Coolidge signed the bill approving the Boulder Canyon Project—so called because it was initially to be built in Boulder Canyon. The final go-ahead for construction was then given in July 1930, under the watchful eye of newly-elected President Herbert Hoover.

The logistics of building the dam were mind-boggling. Engineers had to divert the powerful Colorado River through more than 3 miles (4.8 km) of 50-foot (15.2 m) tunnels, driven straight through the canyon walls. Then they poured millions of cubic yards of concrete in a series of smaller blocks. The river needed to be diverted for two years, and part of the riverbed was excavated down to the bedrock.

Before construction could begin, loose rock—created by erosion—had to be removed from the canyon walls. Men called "high-scalers" were brought in for the job. Rappelling down the canyon walls on ropes, they stripped away the loose rock with jackhammers and dynamite. It was dangerous, hard work and claimed many of the 96 people who died building the dam. The first person to die in the construction of Hoover Dam was J. G. Tierney—a surveyor who drowned on December 20, 1922. His son, Patrick W. Tierney, died 13 years later—to the day—and was one of the last men to die working on the dam.

Six Companies, Inc. won the contract to build the dam, and since nothing

Opposite: A close-up of eight of the 17 hydroelectric generators in the U-shaped base of the dam.

Left: US Highway 93 crossing the top of the Hoover Dam between the two sides of the canyon.

Over: A view down from the top of the dam to the U-shaped base housing the turbines on the Colorado River side.

as large as Hoover Dam had ever been constructed, its engineers had to invent many of their techniques as they went along. The first concrete was poured into the dam in June 1933, but instead of pouring it all as a single mass of concrete, the engineers poured individual columns. They also used cooling pipes—stuck into the wet concrete—to chill the concrete as it was poured. The reason for this was the heat generated by concrete as it "cures," or sets. Engineers had calculated that if poured as a single mass, and without cooling, it would have taken up to 125 years to set! According to experts, the concrete is still curing and gaining in strength every day.

Six Companies also had to provide housing for 80 percent of its employees. Las Vegas, with its notorious reputation, was out of the question. So instead, a new town, Boulder City, was to be built 20 miles (32 km) away. With over 5,000 men on the payroll at the height

of construction, the waiting list for a Six Companies house was very long.

However, the construction schedule for the dam was speeded up to create more jobs as the Great Depression began to bite. As a result, the town was not ready when the first workers arrived on site in early 1931. Instead, they were housed in a temporary camp called Ragtown.

Obviously, these living conditions were not acceptable in the searing desert heat, and disgruntlement grew. Coupled with the dangerous working conditions, including carbon monoxide poisoning from the machinery, conditions were bad enough to push the dam workers to strike in August 1931.

Six Companies dealt with the industrial action harshly, sending in armed strikebreakers. But, the strike did spur the company into finishing the construction of Boulder City, and by

the spring of 1932, Ragtown had been abandoned. However, in the Prohibition era, there were sacrifices to be made to live in Boulder City—during construction of the dam, gambling, hard liquor, and prostitution were not permitted. To this day, Boulder City is one of only two towns in Nevada not to allow gambling.

Besides being a magnificent testament to the men who designed and built it, Hoover Dam is still one of the US's largest hydroelectric plants—helping to provide clean energy to the states of Nevada, Arizona, and California. Another of the dam's great legacies is the invention of the hard hat. After numerous fatal accidents, the high-scalers began dipping their hats in coal tar, causing them to harden. Eventually, Six Companies commissioned commercially-made "hard hats"—something construction workers all over the world today can be thankful for.

London Eye

The London Eye is located on the River Thames in London. One of Great Britain's most popular tourist attractions, it welcomes an estimated 4 million visitors a year.

Above: The London Eye seen from the north bank of the Thames, almost opposite the Prime Minister's residence at 10 Downing Street.

Officially known as the British Airways London Eye, and on occasion as the Millennium Wheel, the London Eye has become one of London's most-loved landmarks since it was built just a few years ago.

Already, the London Eye has become at least as famous as another legendary Ferris wheel, the Prater in Vienna, Austria. However, it took more than a century for the Prater to make its mark on history—while the Eye has seemingly achieved that feat almost overnight.

The world's largest observation wheel when it was completed, the Eye is a majestic structure of both function and form—beautiful to look at and beautiful to look out from. It is 93 feet (28 m) higher than the wheel at Yokohama Bay in Japan, which had been the world's tallest. The Singapore Flyer, when it opens in March 2008, will become the tallest observation wheel at 541 feet (165 m).

Those lucky enough to take a ride—or a "flight," as they are known—on the virtually noiseless and vibration-less wheel are rewarded with views of up to a distance of 25 miles (40 km) on a clear day. These vistas can stretch as far as Windsor Castle to the west of the Eye and always reveal parts of the city you simply cannot see from the ground—for example, the back garden of the British Prime Minister's residence at 10 Downing Street.

A remarkable feat of modern engineering, standing a towering 450 feet (135 m) high and weighing 1,600 tons, the Eye is located on the South Bank of the River Thames, in the London Borough of Lambeth. One of Great Britain's most popular tourist attractions, it welcomes an estimated 4 million visitors a year. Only the British Museum and Tate Modern art museum attract more people—with 4.6 million visitors each. The Eye has also won over 70 awards for national and international tourism, outstanding architectural quality, regeneration, and engineering achievement.

The Eye can carry around 15,000 visitors a day and towers above the traditional London skyline, yet still complements other landmarks including The Houses of Parliament and St. Paul's Cathedral.

Left: Some of the capsules, or "pods," seen from underneath.

Built in 1999, and designed by British husband-and-wife team David Marks and Julia Barfield, of Marks Barfield Architects, the London Eye was arguably the most impressive structure built in the UK to mark the beginning of the 21st century. Initially, the idea was for people to be able to ride on the Eye on New Year's Eve 1999 to welcome the new millennium. But its eventual opening to the public was not without problems.

Because of its vast size and inner-city location, the only way to assemble the wheel was to do so on the River Thames. A large number of booms, forming a floating barrier on the busy waterway, kept boats away. Once these were in place, sections of the Eye were then floated up the river on barges and assembled horizontally on pontoons out toward the middle of the great river.

However, the first attempt to haul the wheel into place—using massive cranes and pulley systems—ended in failure when a cable snapped and sent the wheel crashing back into the Thames.

After that setback, the next attempt saw the wheel raised into an upright

Previous: A close-up of the vast cables holding the wheel in place.

Above and Right: The London Eye is often the focal point of celebrations in the city.

position at two degrees per hour
until it reached 65 degrees. It was
left in that position for a week while
engineers prepared for the second
phase of the lift.

Once the wheel was finally hauled
into place in October 1999, safety
concerns and problems with a clutch
mechanism delayed the opening to the
public still further. Despite the delay,
it provided a spectacular backdrop
to the millennium firework display on
New Year's Day 2000, just after it
was officially opened by Prime
Minister Tony Blair.

People were finally allowed onboard
to experience the magnificent views in
March 2000, just three months behind
schedule. Nevertheless, the structure
was an instant hit.

To get to that stage, the Eye was
a great example of international
cooperation and expertise. Unlike
earlier wheels, which relied on trusses
and braces for strength and stability,
the Eye used 3.7 miles (6 km) of steel
cables imported from Italy to achieve
its rigid circular shape. The steel
frame was built in the Netherlands,
and other parts of the wheel were

manufactured in the Czech Republic
and Germany.

The wheel has 32 sealed, air-
conditioned capsules weighing 10 tons
each and capable of carrying up to
25 people with one revolution taking
30 minutes. The capsules represent the
32 boroughs of London.

The London Eye uses two types of
cables—wheel cables and backstay
cables. The wheel cables include 16
rim rotation cables, and 64 spoke
cables, which make it very similar to a
bicycle wheel. There are six backstay

Right: The spokes of the London Eye and its main supporting structure.

Over: A beautiful view of the London Eye from underneath—imagine what it's like on board!

cables, which are located in the "compression foundation," or holding structure, that keeps this wheel vertical.

The compression foundation is situated underneath the massive A-frame legs, an incredible feature of the construction in Jubilee Gardens. It took 2,200 tons of concrete and 44 concrete piles—each 108 feet (33 m) deep—to anchor the entire structure. The tension foundation, holding the backstay cables, required 1,200 tons of concrete.

The prominence of the wheel in the heart of the capital has also attracted many a protester, keen to scale its heights and fly banners for a cause. This has caused consternation for its operators, who have been forced to halt the ride because of safety fears.

One person who got permission to clamber onto the outside of the construction, however, was American magician David Blaine. On August 28, 2003, he famously stood on one of the capsules, as it went around for a full 30-minute rotation. Blaine did this in preparation for his "Above the Below," 44-day endurance stunt in London, during which he lived—without any

food—in an acrylic box in front of London's City Hall. Some observers wished he had just stuck to the Eye.

Blaine could straddle a passenger capsule with ease for the 30-minute trip thanks to its unique design. The Eye's capsules are suspended, but, thanks to gimbals—triple rings that pivot on each other—fixed on the outside of the main rim, the capsules turn under gravity, thereby allowing a spectacular 360-degree panorama at the top.

Each capsule is entirely see-through, with the exception of the floor, and inscriptions inside inform the visitors where North, South, East, and West lie from their view—not a privilege extended to Mr. Blaine. The wheel turns slowly enough to allow anyone—including children or the elderly—to step on and off the capsules, onto the wooden deck of the landing piers, with ease.

Special packages are available for romantic types who would like to pop the question to their sweethearts with champagne and chocolates, and a capsule all to themselves. Surrounded by the romantic ambience of soaring above one of the world's great cities,

who could resist such a proposal? The London Eye has also featured in numerous television programs and films since its opening, further confirming its status as an iconic feature of London's skyline. Whether serving as a backdrop to action on the Thames or as part of the set for exciting scenes played out within the confines of one of its glass capsules, the Eye has certainly caught the imagination of many directors.

For Marks Barfield, the architects of the project, it was important to create an inviting public space surrounding the base of the structure. The area surrounding the entrance to the London Eye offers space for visitors to take photos, laze around on the grass, and enjoy a picnic. The increased visitor traffic has contributed to a regeneration of the local area.

Despite its impressive design and engineering, the awards and the plaudits thrown its way, the most important factor in the continued success of the London Eye is the fact that people simply love it. Those lucky enough to have "flown" on it will understand why.

CN Tower, Toronto

One of the seven modern Wonders of the World, the CN Tower is the world's tallest freestanding structure on land. It is also a hub for telecommunications and major tourist attraction in Toronto, Canada's largest city.

Above: Since its completion in 1976, the elegant CN Tower has dominated the Toronto skyline as a Canadian icon.

The definitive building on the Toronto skyline, the CN Tower (or Canadian National Tower) is Canada's most celebrated icon. It is also officially one of the modern Seven Wonders of the World, as decreed by the American Society of Civil Engineers. Reaching an astonishing 1,815 feet (553 m), or

the equivalent of 181 stories, it is the world's tallest freestanding structure on land, as well as being a working telecommunications hub and the center of tourism in Toronto.

Located in the heart of the city's Entertainment District, on the north

shore of Lake Ontario, some 2 million people a year have visited the building since it opened in June 1976. The main attraction is the stunning view from a height twice that of the Eiffel Tower.

From the tower's Sky Pod—the highest public observation deck in the world

Left: The CN Tower is a dizzying 1815 feet (553 m) high, the equivalent of 181 stories.

at 1,465 feet (447 m)—on a clear day you can see up to 75 miles (120 km) away to the city of Rochester, New York, and to the mist rising from Niagara Falls. Alternatively, you can test your nerve and look down at the streets below by standing on a glass platform 1,122 feet (343 m) above the ground.

In all, it cost Can$63 million ($54 million), or around Can$300 million ($260 million) in today's money to build the tower, and yet the costs were paid back in just 15 years. It took just over 1,500 people to construct the tower in only 40 months.

A number of serious considerations had to be made when constructing a tower of this height—not least the natural threats. As a result, it's designed to withstand an earthquake of 8.5 on the Richter scale and can tolerate winds of up to 260 mph (420 km/h). In winds of over 120 mph, however, the tower can sway up to 11 feet (3.3 m) from its center at the Sky Pod, and the antenna can sway up to 31 feet (9.4 m). However, the tower is equipped to withstand such movements with ease.

CN Tower, Toronto

Previous: The Toronto skyline seen from the shores of Lake Ontario.

Above and Right: The Sky Pod of the CN Tower emerging from the treetops of Toronto and dwarfing other buildings.

As if that weren't enough, the CN Tower is struck by lightning at least 40 to 50 times a year—more frequently than any other structure in the city. However, since opening it hasn't suffered any damage from lightning strikes since the charge is conducted straight to the ground.

Another impressive aspect of the CN Tower is its internal metal staircase of 2,579 steps up to the Sky Pod—the tallest metal staircase on earth. These stairs are intended for emergency use and are usually not open to the public, but three times a year the building hosts charity stair-climb events.

It takes on average 30 minutes to scale the stairs, but the fastest climb on record is 7 minutes and 52 seconds, a feat accomplished in 1989 by Brendan Keenoy, an Ontario Provincial police officer. The fastest record for a woman was set by Chrissy Redden, who climbed the stairs in 11 minutes and 52 seconds in 2000.

The tower's birth, however, had a more practical purpose. The construction boom in Toronto in the 1960s and early 1970s transformed the previously low-rise skyline with a host of skyscrapers, especially in the downtown area. Although a sign of progress in the city, these new buildings hampered communications by blocking or reflecting various signals from radio and TV broadcasts as they loomed above existing transmitters.

In 1968, Canadian National Railway (CN) decided that a good way around this would be to build a large TV and radio communications platform as part of a tower taller than any other in the world. As well as solving communications problems in Toronto, it would demonstrate the strength of Canadian industry.

Construction finally started in February 1973 with massive excavations at the tower base for the foundations. By the time the foundations were complete—in just four months—62,000 tons of dirt and shale had been removed to a depth of 50 feet (15 m).

The tower was finished on April 2, 1975, after 40 months of construction, officially capturing the height record from Moscow's Ostankino Tower.

However, it is not likely to hold this record for long. The Burj Dubai looks set to be the first to steal the CN Tower's crown, and it is already the tallest building in the Middle East. Once finished, it will be 2,625 feet (800 m) high—or just shy of half a mile. But, even when the CN inevitably loses its place in the record books, nothing will ever diminish its rightful status as one of the true architectural wonders of the world.

Below: A view of the CN Tower from one of Toronto's numerous parks.

Over: The CN Tower and the city skyline seen from Toronto Island Park.

Right: Liberty's seven-pointed crown, representing the seven seas and the seven continents, pierces the sky.

Statue of Liberty

The famous Statue of Liberty was a gift presented by the French nation to the people of the United States in honor of the friendship between the two countries. It stands as a symbol of hope, liberty, and freedom recognized throughout the world.

The Statue of Liberty, one of the most widely recognized icons in the world, is a statue located on Ellis Island in Jersey City. The statue was given to the United States in 1886 by the Paris-based Union Franco-Americaine (Franco-American Union). It is situated in the mouth of the Hudson River in New York Harbor. The copper statue was built over a skeleton framework of steel, with the flame of the torch section coated in gold leaf. The statue itself stands just over 151 feet (46 m) tall. Its construction required the use of 225 tons of copper, while the foundation is made of granite and stands another 154 feet (47 m) tall. The statue is of a woman dressed in a flowing robe and wearing a seven-point spiked crown. Cradled in her left arm is a stone tablet that reads, "JULY IV MDCCLXXVI" (July 4, 1776) which commemorates the date of the United States Declaration of Independence. In her right outstretched hand, she holds a torch—known as the Flame of Liberty. The grand statue was a gift presented by the French people to the American people in honor of the friendship between the two countries. It stands as a symbol of liberty and individual freedom recognized throughout the world.

The creator and sculptor of the Statue of Liberty was Frédéric-Auguste Bartholdi. At the age of 31, Bartholdi was already a well-known sculptor from Colmar, a French town located in the eastern province of Alsace. While attending a dinner party in 1865, hosted by Edouard René Lefebvre de Laboulaye, a scholar of the time, Bartholdi was captured by the notion of creating a great monument to be given to the American people. The subjects of discussion that evening had been about oppressive regime of Napoleon III, and the admiration felt for the Americans' success in creating a democratic government and abolishing slavery at the end of the Civil War. "Wouldn't it be wonderful if people in France gave the United States a great monument as a lasting memorial to their independence and thereby showed that the French government was also dedicated to the idea of human liberty?" It was several years later that Bartholdi remembered the idea of the monument. He wrote that Laboulaye's idea "interested me so deeply that it remained fixed in my memory."

Though Bartholdi had begun his career as a painter, he eventually became

Above: The statue's gold leaf flame represents enlightenment and freedom from oppression.

Above: The bright green color of the oxidized copper provides a contrast to the warm golden glow of the pedestal's stonework.

Right: A symbol of strength and hope.

Over: The statue, positioned at the edge of the city, is intended to offer a welcome to New York's immigrants.

famous for his expertise as a sculptor. Even though Bartholdi had always created huge statues, it was only after a trip to Egypt that he expanded his creative perspective to colossal proportions. Strongly influenced by the magnitude of the Pyramids and the Sphinx, Bartholdi was ready for the next awesome step up as he considered his Liberty sculpture.

At the urging of Laboulaye, Bartholdi sailed to the United States with the proposal to create the Statue of Liberty. Laboulaye had said, "Propose to our friends over there to make with us a monument, a common work, in remembrance of the ancient friendship of France and the United States. [If] you find a plan that will excite public enthusiasm, we are convinced that it will be successful on both continents, and we will do a work that will have far-reaching moral effect."

Bartholdi considered New York Harbor to be the perfect location for the statue. It was "where people get their first view of the New World," he wrote. "I've found an admirable spot. It is Bedloe Island, in the middle of the bay…the island belongs to the government; it's on national territory, belonging to all the states, just opposite the Narrows, which are, so to speak, the gateway to America."

Due to the expense of the project, it was decided that France and America should share the cost. France would pay for the statue and America would pay for the pedestal and foundation for the statue. Comprised of members from both

countries, a fund-raising committee, the Franco-American Union, was formed. They staged many elaborate fund-raising events, but the money flow was extremely slow. Although enough money was collected to begin the work on the statue, it was apparent that it would not be finished in time for America's 100th anniversary celebration.

Famous engineer Alexandre-Gustave Eiffel was chosen as the designer for the intricate skeleton for the statue. Eiffel was already known for his iron railroad bridges, and would eventually be best known for his design of the Eiffel Tower.

In an effort to raise the much-needed funds to complete the statue, the Franco-American Union committee decided to create a lottery, with the prizes being two Bartholdi sculptures. The committee also issued signed and numbered clay models of the statue to be sold in both France and the United States. By the end of 1879, they had raised approximately 250,000 French francs, the equivalent of $750,000 for the construction of the statue.

By 1884, Bartholdi was putting the finishing touches to the statue. Laboulaye never saw the realization of his dream. In May 1883, he died from a heart ailment. The statue was finally unveiled in Paris, at a grand ceremony attended by French Prime Minister Jules Ferry and U.S. Ambassador Morton. The statue was then dismantled in anticipation of shipping it to America, but it remained in Paris until the spring of 1885.

As the Statue of Liberty neared completion, little money had been raised for the American phase of the project. By 1884, only $182,491 had been collected, while $179,624 had already been spent. The American press had been critical of the project, and its expense, from the beginning. It was not until Joseph Pulitzer became involved that fund-raising efforts improved. Pulitzer saw an opportunity to increase his newspaper's circulation and to be able to criticize the wealthy for their lack of support of the monument project. Circulation of the *World* newspaper increased to nearly 50,000 copies when Pulitzer promised to print the name of every contributor to the fund-raising for the pedestal and base for the statue. Pulitzer wrote: "The World is the people's paper and it now appeals to the people to come forward and raise the money (for the statue's pedestal)."

African-American newspapers embraced the fund-raising cause, encouraging their readers to donate money because the statue would be a commemoration of the end of slavery. Everyone from schoolchildren to grandmothers gave pennies and single dollars to help reach the goal of $100,000 set by Pulitzer.

The Statue of Liberty arrived on Bedloe Island in 214 crates on June 15, 1885. The August 11 front page of the *World* displayed a headline of "ONE HUNDRED THOUSAND DOLLARS!" Thanks to Joseph Pulitzer's support—through his newspaper—and the individual contributions of over 120,000 people, the statue's fund-

raising goal had not only been reached, but had slightly exceeded the proposed amount. In May 1886 the process of assembling the Liberty statue, and hoisting it to its final resting place, began. It took a total of six months to place the statue onto its base and pedestal. On October 25, 1886, the Statue of Liberty was unveiled and dedicated. Among the many dignitaries attending the ceremony was President Grover Cleveland, his cabinet, and the Governor of New York and his staff.

During the parade leading to the dedication ceremony for the statue, office boys began unrolling ticker tape and tossing it out of the upper windows along the parade route. This began the tradition of ticker tape parades in New York.

In 1903, one of the changes to the pedestal was the inclusion of a bronze plaque bearing the poem, "The New Colossus," written by Emma Lazarus to raise funds for the construction of the statue's pedestal.

Not like the brazen giant of Greek fame,
With conquering limbs astride from land to land:
Here at our sea-washed, sunset gates shall stand
A mighty woman with a torch, whose flame
Is the imprisoned lightning, and her name
Mother of Exiles. From her beacon-hand
Glows world-wide welcome; her mild eyes command
The air-bridged harbor that twin cities frame.
Keep, ancient lands, your, storied pomp!" cries she
With silent lips. "Give me your tired, your poor,
Your huddled masses yearning to breathe free,
The wretched refuse of your teeming shore.
Send these, the homeless, tempest-tost, to me,
I lift my lamp beside the gold door!"

In 1916, further funds were raised for floodlights to illuminate the statue at night. In 1924, President Calvin Coolidge declared the Statue of Liberty a national monument, and a few years later, the National Park Service took over the administration and maintenance of the statue.

The Franco-American Committee for the Restoration of the Statue of Liberty, which was established in 1981, did a survey of the statue, and discovered that it was in great need of restorative work. Through the newly formed Statue of Liberty-Ellis Island Foundation, fund-raising efforts for the massive project began. The foundation raised $295 million, with $86 million going directly into the restoration work on the statue itself.

In a ceremony that was televised around the world, the United States celebrated the very special centennial of the Statue of Liberty on July 4, 1986. President Ronald Reagan said during the ceremony, "We are the keeper of the Flame of Liberty; we hold it high for the world to see."

Below and Left: The tablet in Liberty's left arm bears the date of the country's emancipation, July 1776.

Over: Liberty's green hue is a fitting statement of the country's new birth as an independent nation.

St. Louis Gateway Arch

The sleek design of the St. Louis Gateway Arch was created as a symbol of St. Louis' important role in the westward expansion of the United States in the 19th century. The design is timeless—looking as modern and futuristic now as it did at the time of its completion in 1965.

Above and Opposite: The Gateway Arch, opened in 1965 to commemorate Thomas Jefferson and the westward expansion of the US.

Over: The stainless steel St. Louis Gateway Arch gleaming in the sunshine.

In 1935, the St. Louis riverfront was selected as the site for a monument commemorating the westward expansion of the United States in the 19th century. The property was purchased, and the site was cleared of buildings in preparation of the monument construction. Construction on the monument was halted due to World War II. But in 1947, the public-minded Jefferson National Expansion Memorial Association revived the project, and held a national competition for the creation of an appropriate design for the memorial. Finnish-American architect Eero Saarinen and his father, Eliel Saarinen, both entered the memorial project competition. When the time came for the committee to announce the winner of the design competition, they spoke with the senior Saarinen. Upon hearing that his design had been chosen, the architect broke out champagne in celebration. While celebrating he received another call from the judges who apologized. The winner of the competition was *Eero* Saarinen. When the senior Saarinen heard that his son was the winner, he served another bottle of champagne to celebrate his son winning the

competition. The junior Saarinen already had several world-renowned architectural creations to his credit, such as the TWA Flight Center in New York, John Deere Headquarters, IBM Headquarters, and the CBS Headquarters. He was also the creator of the Tulip Chair as well as many other organic types of furniture.

Eero Saarinen, now considered one of the masters of 20th-century architecture, was highly criticized during his lifetime for having no identifiable style. He adapted his modernistic design vision to each client and project. The winning design for the memorial in St. Louis was like nothing else that Saarinen had designed to date. The design was that of an inverted catenary arch, though not a pure catenary. He preferred a slightly more elongated arch that was thinner toward its peak. Catenary is the curve shape produced when a flexible hanging chain or cable is supported at its ends and acted upon by the uniform gravitational force of its own weight. The inverted catenary is an ideal form for an arch supporting only itself. There is no significant shear

force present at the joints, as long as the individual elements—whose contacting surfaces are perpendicular to the curve of the arch—and the thrust into the ground follow directly along the line of the arch. To develop his design, Saarinen had the help of German-American structural engineer Hannskarl Bandel. Bandel had been the contributing "structural force" on such projects as the Ford Foundation Headquarters, The Kennedy Center for the Performing Arts in Washington, D.C., and the cylindrical Marina Towers in Chicago, Illinois. In later life, he created an innovative study for the NASA Mars Pathfinder project, in which he designed trusses to be assembled without tools in zero gravity conditions. Saarinen held up a chain in an attempt to show Bandel his idea for the arch design. Bandel asked for the chain, returning in a few days with the solution. By replacing the constant size of the chain cylinders with graduated links, Bandel was able to achieve the "soaring" effect to Saarinen's arch design. Saarinen wanted to create "...a monument that would have a lasting significance and would be a landmark of our time.

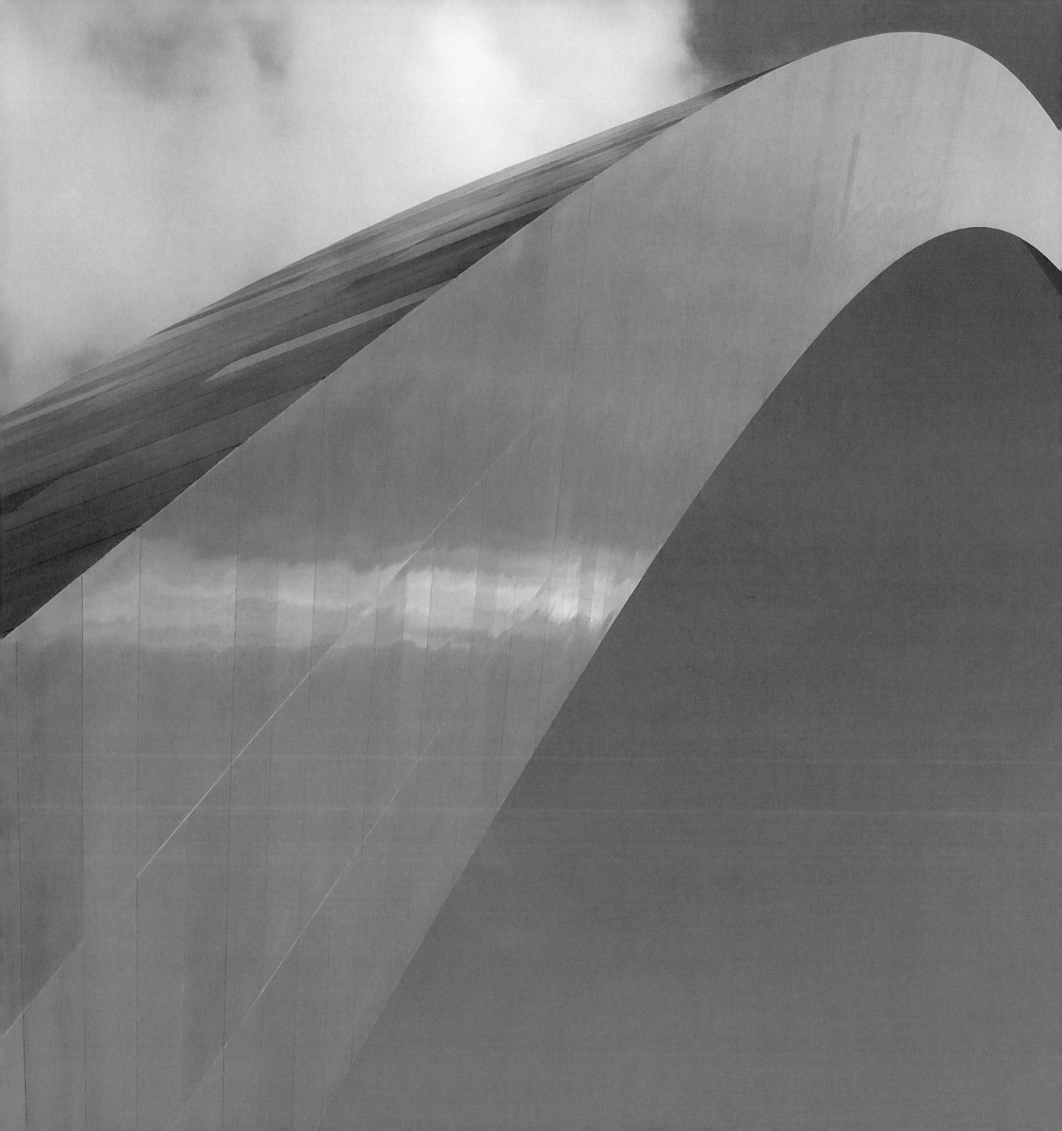

*Above and Right: The 630-foot St. Louis
Gateway Arch in the Jefferson National
Expansion Memorial Park on the banks of
the Mississippi River.*

*Over: The United States' tallest national
memorial towers over the city of St. Louis.*

Neither an obelisk nor a rectangular box nor a dome seemed right on this site for this purpose. But here at the edge of the Mississippi River a great arch seemed right." By the time construction of the Arch began in 1963, the location was moved closer inland to avoid future problems from flooding from the Mississippi River. The sleek arch design was symbolic of St. Louis's role as an important part of the gateway opening up not only the new western United States in the 19th century, but also a gateway symbolizing St. Louis' importance in the future as well. The design is timeless—looking as modern and futuristic now as it did at the time of its completion in 1965.

Four years before the completion of the arch, designer Saarinen died from a brain tumor. Shortly before his death, he realized that a power lift system should be created in order to avoid the thousand-stair climb to reach the top. After unsuccessful meetings with several elevator designers, he hired college dropout Richard Bowser to solve the problem. Bowser was the inventor of the Bowser Parking System, a system that had elevators traveling vertically, horizontally, and diagonally in parking garages. Skeptical St. Louis city leaders gave Bowser only two weeks to come up with a solution for the elevator system in the arch. The system he designed was a tram combined with an elevator cable-lift system with gimbaled cars. Its function is similar to that of Ferris wheel gondolas. Gimbals are a set of three

metal rings that pivot on each other, thereby maintaining the object being supported on a horizontal plane, similar to a ship's compass.

As the tallest national monument in the United States, the Gateway Arch stands 630 feet (192 m) tall and goes from 54 feet (16 m) wide at the base to 17 feet (5.1 m) wide at the top of the monument. Each of its walls consists of a stainless steel covering over reinforced concrete from the ground level up to 300 feet (91.4 m). Carbon steel and rebars (ridged steel bars) are used from 300 feet (91.4 m) up to the peak of the arch. The interior of the arch is hollow and contains a unique transport system that leads to an observation deck at the top. Two emergency stairwells, consisting of 1076 stairs, were created should the tram system fail to work. Passengers in groups of five enter a horizontal cylindrical compartment containing five seats. Due to the shape of the car, the compartments have sloped ceilings that are low enough to force taller riders to lean forward while seated. It is usually recommended that the tallest of the five passengers sit in the center position and facing the door. There are eight compartments linked together to form a train. Each leg of the arch has a capacity of forty passengers, which means that eighty people can be transported at a time. Each compartment maintains a correct level by rotating, which permits them to maintain a proper orientation while the whole train travels on curved

tracks up one leg of the arch. It takes four minutes to reach the top of the arch, and three minutes for the return trip back down to earth. During the trip, passengers have a view of the interior of the arch through narrow glass panels in the car doors. Riders exit the compartment near the top of the arch climbing a slight grade to enter the arched observation deck. From the observation deck, through small windows not visible from the ground level, passengers can see the Mississippi River and across to Illinois. The tram system carries 200 to 225 passengers per hour.

The system's inventor, Richard Bowser, served with the National Park Service maintenance staff at the Arch until 1972. Thanks to his innovative design and the full-time maintenance staff, the Arch trains have continued to operate safely and efficiently for over 35 years. Since 9/11, visitors must pass through security checkpoints at each entrance to the Arch before being allowed to access the Visitor Centers, which are located at the base of each leg. As a result of the Congressional mandate to establish a Counter-Terrorism Program at the park, the National Park Service used funds to increase security by purchasing metal detectors, closed-circuit cameras, and x-ray equipment for visitor screening.

It is hardly surprising that over 25 million people have visited St. Louis's spectacular Gateway Arch. After all, it is one of the great architectural wonders of the world.

Christ the Redeemer, Rio

The wide-open arms of the Christ the Redeemer statue, which towers above the Brazilian city of Rio de Janeiro, simultaneously represent Christ's universal compassion and the city's openhearted, hospitable people.

Rising triumphant from the top of Rio de Janeiro's Corcovado Mountain, the magnificent statue of Christ the Redeemer (*Cristo Redentor*) watches over the city with a benevolent, all-encompassing gaze. Its wide-open arms are simultaneously symbolic of Christ's universal compassion and of the city's open-hearted, hospitable people. The statue seems to belong to the rock out of which it rises, to be an integral part of the city. Yet it has traveled a long journey from the first spark of inspiration back in the 1850s. It was a Catholic priest, Pedro Maria Boss, who first suggested the erection of a religious monument on Corcovado (literally, "hunchback"). But he had difficulty persuading the authorities, particularly Princess Isabel of Portugal, whom he approached for funding. The separation of Church and State—an inevitable result of Brazil's transformation into a Republic in 1889—made the idea of a huge religious statue gracing the capital even less likely. The notion was deemed inappropriate, even distasteful, in the new secular climate.

However, the idea reappeared in 1921, from the same quarters—the Catholic Church—but this time, it had the full backing of the Archdiocese of Rio de Janeiro. The money for the statue was raised largely by Brazil's wealthier Catholics, and before long, designs were being put forward. One of the designs considered was Christ holding a globe, but the concept of the Redeemer seemed to be more evocative of the Christian ethos of love and forgiveness. The statue was designed by a Brazilian engineer, Heitor da Costa, and created by French-Polish sculptor Paul Landowski. A graduate of the French National Academy, Landowski won the Prix de Rome—a prestigious fine arts award—in 1900 with his statue of David, and he went on to furnish the cities of Europe with many more imposing statues. Christ the Redeemer was constructed using reinforced concrete—rather than the stainless steel favored by the Art Deco movement—with an outer shell of soapstone, chosen for its softness and resilience.

Fortunately, given the challenging nature of the construction project, a railway already ran up the steep mountainside. Otherwise the builders would have faced enormous difficulties getting the materials in place. The foundation stone was laid on April 22, 1922, and the monument was finally inaugurated on October 12, 1931, in a grandiose ceremony led by president Getúlio Vargas. The plan was for the climax of the ceremony to involve a stunning light show, which would be switched on by Guglielmo Marconi from his yacht in Naples. This would have been an apt coupling as Marconi had earned his own place at the cutting edge of innovation with his invention of the radio. Furthermore, the Art Deco movement was itself a celebration of the age of modern machinery. However, adverse weather conditions thwarted this romantic plan, and in the end, the lights had to be switched on manually by laborers on site.

The Art Deco movement was at its height when Christ the Redeemer

Left: Art Deco touches are evident in the flatness and thick ribbing of the garment.

Over: The open arms of forgiveness.

was designed. An amalgamation of various other artistic movements such as Cubism, Modernism, Bauhaus, and Art Nouveau, Art Deco is essentially about elegance and streamlined functionality. The almost "primitive" look brought about by the simple, clean lines and bold, oversized, obvious shapes is a major part of the statue's attraction, tapping into a childlike need for reassuring order and rightness. The sweeping curves and stepped forms, together with the statue's immense size, create the sense of paternal security—another of its features. The overall sense is that things are as they should be.

Recent modernizations of the statue include a panoramic elevator and a motorized staircase to improve access. A small chapel has also been consecrated in the benevolent shadow of the statue, so that Catholics can be married and baptized under its protective gaze. The statue can be seen from all corners of the capital city, and its

impact is undeniably dramatic, with Christ's large embrace a constant reminder of universal love.

Visitors to Rio can enjoy a trip up the Corcovado Mountain through the world's largest urban forest. From the top of the mountain, a 360-degree panorama opens up, encompassing the splendor of Rio's beaches, forests, the Botanic Garden, Macarana Stadium, Rio Niteroi Bridge, and the Jockey Club.

Experienced rock climbers can eschew the trains and escalators, and opt instead for one of nearly 50 climbing routes up the side of the mountain. Be warned, though— these are not hiking trails, and serious rock-climbing equipment is required!

However visitors choose to make the ascent, no stay in Rio de Janeiro would be complete without a trip to the top of Corcovado Mountain to appreciate this modern wonder of the world up close.

Left: Christ the Redeemer stands atop a misty Corcovado mountain.

Over: Close-up of the face of compassion, carved in soapstone.

Grand Central Station

Grand Central Station opened in 1913 to the great delight and excitement of New York City residents. From then on, the city began its transformation into a buzzing metropolis and one of the frontrunners in modern urban advance.

Back in the 19th century, out of the smoke-choked fug of an industrialized and entirely unrecognizable Park Avenue, a railroad emerged which was to transform New York City into a sparkling metropolis. The first train line to cut a path through the city was the New York and Harlem Railroad. It was constructed in 1831, amidst the factories, breweries, and slaughterhouses that daily pumped their thick fumes into an air filled with the hum of machinery. During the 1840s, rival services began to emerge, demanding a greater supply of terminals and stations throughout the city. At this point in history, the railroad was a jumble of horse-drawn and steam-powered engines, but the horse was clearly on its way out. Increasingly, steam-powered locomotives were being banned from built-up residential areas after complaints about excessive noise and pollution. Once steam trains were no longer allowed to run beyond 42nd Street, a new terminal was needed to accommodate the curtailed lines. Cue the arrival of Grand Central Station.

In 1864, the shipping magnate Cornelius Vanderbilt entered the field when he acquired the Hudson River Railroad. He soon began to expand his empire, adding further railroads to his holdings and ultimately purchasing significant land on the East Side in order to build the Grand Central Depot. Three separate lines terminated at this building, which was designed by John B. Snook in 1871 and then further expanded by architects Bradford Lee Gilbert and Samuel Huckel, Jr. The result was a remarkably striking building whose unique feature was a vast glass and steel train shed. Aside from its dramatic impact, it was also an admirable feat of engineering and boldly progressive for its time. However, impressive as it was, it was not to last, and the glass roof eventually collapsed under the weight of a New York blizzard on the very same day that Cornelius Vanderbilt died. What really made this building stand out, however, was its daring ornamentation, which included a magnificent pair of cast-iron eagles—with a wingspan of 13 feet (3.9 m)—adorning the station's facade.

However, by this time, the steam locomotive had had its day of glory, and it was now being consigned to the past.

Opposite: Detail of the ornate classical ornamentation that graces the terminal building.

Left and Over: The opal face of the famous four-faced clock, which stands in the main concourse.

There was no escaping the advance of technology, and electric trains were the story of the future. It took a horrific train accident, which killed 17 passengers in the dense smoke of Park Avenue Tunnel, to banish the steam train forever from New York's streets. In order to make way for the new electric trains, the existing Grand Central Station had to be completely destroyed and rebuilt again from scratch. Its rebirth was the work of engineer William J. Wilgus. Transforming the original railroads to accommodate electric trains was a punishingly expensive business, which involved excavating for miles, deep into the layers of bedrock beneath Manhattan. But Wilgus came up with a clever solution—to sell off the paved-over railroad to property developers at premium prices. It was from this sale that city landmarks such as the Waldorf-Astoria Hotel and the Chrysler Building were born.

A competition was launched for the design of the new station, and the final result brought about a collaboration between two separate firms—Reed and Stem of St. Paul, Minnesota, and Warren and Wetmore of New York City. Both firms boasted architects who were related to members of the selection committee. It took 10 years to bring the new station to life, largely due to the enormous time and effort involved in excavating so deep below ground level. Grand Central Station reopened in 1913 to the great delight and excitement of New York City residents, and from then on, the city began its transformation into a buzzing metropolis and one of the frontrunners in modern urban

advance. During the 1920s, grand hotels, impressive apartment buildings, and breathtaking skyscrapers began to spring up in the area surrounding Grand Central Station. The station became a microcosm of the city outside, as big names in the world of business and entertainment made their headquarters within its walls. Most notably, CBS had its headquarters here from 1948 to 1964, and the evening news became famous for its shaky pictures caused by the trains rumbling past.

But this was not to be the end of the story. The prosperity of the railways soon began to fade. The automobile was in its ascendancy, and ownership of a car was just one facet of a general rise in individual ownership that could afford to dispense with communal public transport. Another factor in the railway's demise was that the city's population was beginning to spread outwards to the suburbs, and in the age of the car, they traveled there under their own steam. The era of long distance rail travel was in steep decline, and rents around the Manhattan area had been inflated to such an extent (a byproduct, ironically, of Grand Central's former prosperity) that the station was no longer financially viable. Grand Central Station would certainly have been demolished in the 1960s, but for the fortunate stroke of being designated a "landmark" by the newly formed Landmarks Preservation Commission. The building numbered amongst its champions such famous names as Jacqueline Kennedy Onassis, and amidst the various plans to turn it into a commercial skyscraper, the public outrage was strong enough to ensure its

Above: The main concourse, in a quiet hour.

Opposite: Historic and modern meet harmoniously in the newly refurbished station.

Right: Some of the 35,000 commuters who pass through the terminal every week.

Over: The past lives on in artistic details.

preservation. As Mrs. Kennedy Onassis opined: "Is it not cruel to let our city die by degrees, stripped of all her proud monuments, until there will be nothing left of all her history or beauty to inspire our children? This is the time to take a stand, to reverse the tide, so that we won't all end up in a uniform world of steel and glass boxes."

The 1980s and 1990s saw Grand Central Terminal (as it is more properly, though less popularly, called) restored and revitalized by Metro-North and the Metropolitan Transportation Authority. They made the most of the commercial opportunities available, and transformed it into a sophisticated retail experience, complete with cocktail lounge and oyster bar. The process of rebuilding the station to its former glory involved the original quarry in Tennessee that had supplied its stone reopening specifically for the purpose. It stands now as a glittering testament to the railroad's long-serving dedication and unswerving loyalty. Indeed, trains never once stopped running throughout all the years of turmoil. It is, once again, a reflection of its former grandeur and prosperity.

Grand Central has 44 platforms—more than any other station in the world—serving some 67 tracks and around 35,000 passengers a week. But it is remarkable beyond its mere capacity. There are various outstanding features that make this station a beautiful work of architecture, and indeed of art. The main concourse is famous for its four-faced clock which, besides being a romantic meeting point both in reality and in the movies, is also a magnificent

piece of jewelry. Its four faces are made of opal and its value has been estimated at between $10 and $20 million. The clock sits atop a marble and brass stand that houses a secret spiral staircase leading to the information booth below. One aspect of the original station that has been maintained and was revealed during the painstaking renovation of the 1980s is the wonderfully quirky ceiling in the main concourse. The ceiling, with its astronomical theme, was painted in 1912 by the French painter Paul César Helleu. Restoring it involved scraping away a thick black coat of tar and nicotine from the decades of cigarette smoke rising up to its lofty heights. What was revealed was in fact the celestial sphere in reverse. Cynics say that the artist simply painted his image of the constellations back to front by mistake. But the official reason handed down through the generations is that the image was based on a medieval manuscript, which—as was common then—depicted the sky from the "other side", or from God's point of view. A further oddity in the ceiling is that it still bears a "battle wound" from the 1950s, when it was decided that the American Redstone space missile be put on display in the main concourse. There was no way of putting it in place other than lowering it down through the ceiling, and the restorers decided to preserve this hole as a vital piece in the jigsaw of the station's history. Another piece of design history is the Campbell Apartment, a gracious cocktail lounge decorated in the style of a medieval Florentine palace, which was once the office and home of 1920s tycoon John W. Campbell.

Sydney Opera House

The Sydney Opera House is described as an Expressionist modern design, with a series of large precast concrete "shells" forming the roofs of the structure. It is an immediately recognizable symbol of Australia's largest city.

Above: A close-up of some of the millions of tiles on the gleaming white roof of the Sydney Opera House.

Opposite: The giant "sails" on the roof of Sydney Opera House viewed from the waters of the harbor.

Often called the Eighth Wonder of the World, Sydney Opera House is one of the most iconic buildings on the planet and a much-loved emblem of Australia.

It also manages to be somehow timeless and ageless through its unique design, which enhances its surrounding environment rather than detracting from it.

Sited on Bennelong Point, which reaches out into the city's stunning natural harbor, it looks like a great ship at full sail in the azure waters. Sydney Opera House is also understandably the cultural center of the city, if not the entire country. As well as being one of Sydney's most popular tourist attractions, it is also a working arts center and home to numerous arts companies, including the Australian Ballet, the Australian Chamber Orchestra, and Opera Australia, to name but a few.

Opened—to much fanfare and before millions of people—on October 20, 1973, by Queen Elizabeth II, it is somewhat ironic that this Australian

beauty was in fact designed by renowned Danish architect Jorn Utzon.

Before the opera house was built, there was no suitable place in the city to host ballets, concerts, and the like. Instead, these were held at Sydney's Town Hall, but the building was deemed too small and the acoustics not up to scratch.

So, in the late 1940s, Sir Eugene Goossens, the Chief Conductor of the Sydney Symphony Orchestra and Director of the New South Wales Conservatorium of Music, suggested the creation of an opera house. In 1954, the state government finally agreed, and a year later it launched a competition to design what would be the Sydney Opera House. They simultaneously launched an appeal and fund-raising efforts in order to finance its construction.

In the end, they received 233 entries from 32 countries. The criteria specified a large hall, capable of seating 3,000 people, and a small hall for 1,200 people. Each was to be designed for different uses including

full-scale operas, orchestral and choral concerts, and ballet performances.

Utzon's design was declared the winner in 1957, and he flew out to Sydney that year to help supervise the project.

The Fort Macquarie Tram Depot, occupying the site at the time, was demolished in 1958, and formal construction of the Opera House began in March 1959. The project comprised three stages. Stage I (1959–1963) consisted of building the upper podium. Stage II (1963–1967) saw the construction of the outer shells. Stage III (1967–73) consisted of the interior design and construction.

However, at the start of construction, no one could work out quite how to actually build its distinguishing feature—the "sails" on the roof. Initially, the "shells" were planned as a series of parabolas—or bowl shapes—supported by precast concrete ribs. However, engineers Ove Arup & Partners were unable to find an acceptable solution to constructing them.

Utzon was sent back to the drawing board, where he spent a couple of years reworking his vision. The design work on the shells involved one of the earliest uses of computers in structural analysis. This was necessary in order to understand the complex forces the shells would be subjected to. In mid-1961, the design team finally found a solution to the problem: the shells would all be created as sections from a sphere.

By then, work was already running almost a year behind schedule. This was not just because of Utzon's redesign, but also due to inclement weather, unexpected difficulty diverting storm waters, construction beginning before proper drawings had been prepared, and changes in the original contract documents.

However, this was only the start of issues to blight the building's construction. Costs for the venture began escalating out of control, to the extent that the New South Wales government considered halting the project on more than one occasion.

By the end of 1965, the scheduled completion date was almost two years overdue. Then in 1966, the situation reached crisis point. Arguments about cost and interior design grew to such an extent that Utzon resigned. To this day, opinion is still divided as to the roles of the different parties in the project and the eventual resignation of Utzon.

Utzon's resignation caused outrage and a rift amongst Sydney's architects. There were rallies and marches to Sydney Town Hall led by some architects, others resigned in protest and took up other careers including teaching and filmmaking. However, on April 19, 1966, despite the maelstrom of debate, the new architectural team—consisting of Lionel Todd, David Littlemore, and Peter Hall—was appointed.

Major aspects of Utzon's plan were then reviewed. The function of the halls was changed, and two more theatres were also added. The layout of the interiors was altered, and the stage machinery—already designed and fitted inside the major hall—was pulled out and mostly thrown away. In the end, Utzon's interior designs were scrapped completely.

The building was eventually completed in 1973 at a cost of $83 million ($AU 102 million). The original cost estimate, in 1957, was $7 million ($AU 8.6 million), and the original completion date set by the government had been January 26, 1963.

The finished Sydney Opera House is described as an Expressionist modern design, with a series of 2194 large precast concrete "shells" forming the roofs of the structure. Some of the shells weigh up to 15 tons. In all, they weigh more than 27,000 tons and are held together by 217 miles (350 km) of tensioned steel cable. The

highest roof vault is 221 feet (67.3 m) above sea level, and the entire roof structure is covered with over 1 million self-cleaning tiles, which give it its majestic white color. Inside, the building's interior is composed of Australian pink granite, wood, and brush box plywood supplied from northern New South Wales.

The Opera House covers 4.5 acres (1.8 ha) of land, and it is supported on 580 concrete piers sunk down to 82 feet (25 m) below sea level. Its power supply could service a town of 25,000 people.

Annually, 2 million people attend performances here, and 200,000 tourists a year take the guided tours, The Sydney Opera House contains five theatres, five rehearsal studios, two main halls, four restaurants, six bars, and numerous souvenir shops.

Happily, Jorn Utzon is now once again involved with the beloved building he helped create. Beginning in the late 1990s, the Sydney Opera House Trust began to communicate with Utzon in an attempt to effect reconciliation and to secure his involvement in future changes to the building. In 1999, the trust appointed him a design consultant for future work. In 2004, Sydney Opera House opened the first interior space that had been rebuilt to match Utzon's original design. The transformed reception hall was renamed The Utzon Room in his honor.

Above and Opposite: Sydney Opera House, built on Bennelong Point in the city's great harbor to appear like a mighty ship in full sail.

Over: Although self-cleaning, the glazed white granite tiles on the roof of the Opera House still need maintenance occasionally.

Eiffel Tower

Designed by the engineer Gustave Eiffel in 1887, the Eiffel Tower was created to serve as an archway leading to the entrance of a huge fair held in Paris to celebrate the 100th anniversary of the French Revolution. The tower has stood over Paris for much longer than originally anticipated, and now it is hardly possible to imagine the city without its evocative symbol.

The iron archway that is the Eiffel Tower is perhaps the most commonly recognizable structure in the world— so distinctive is its unique and striking design. It is also the most visited of all the world's tourist attractions, with around 6.5 million people making the pilgrimage up its stairs and elevators every year. Once the tallest structure in the world, it can now only claim to be the tallest in Paris. Unsurprisingly, the maintenance on 7300 tons of ironwork reaching up 1,063 feet (324 m) into the sky is no light matter. The entire structure has to be repainted every seven years to protect it from rust corrosion. In addition to that, the tower must be painted in three graded colors from top to bottom in order to maintain the appearance of uniform color. This is because of the optical illusion created by the changing background—the same color looks different against the comparatively light sky from the way it looks against the dark backdrop of the city at ground level.

*Opposite: Boat on the River Seine
alongside the tower.*

*Left: The tower bestrides its neighboring
Trocadero Gardens.*

Designed by the engineer Gustave
Eiffel in 1887, it was to serve as
an archway to the entrance of the
Exposition Universelle (Universal
Exhibition), a huge fair celebrating
the 100th anniversary of the French
Revolution. The Eiffel Tower has
withstood the test of time to an
extent that was never intended in its
inception, and has in fact become
more permanent than could ever
have been expected. The competition
to design the gateway to the Paris
exhibition required that the structure
be easy to dismantle, because it was
only supposed to stand for 20 years.
The Eiffel Tower would have been torn
down in 1909 but for its fortuitous
usefulness in providing excellent
radio communications. During the
Battle of the Marne, Parisian taxis
were dispatched to the front line,
an operation that was coordinated
via signaling from the Eiffel Tower.
From then on, the monument held
a permanent place in the nation's
heart. It comes as something of a
surprise to discover that the icon—now

115

Previous: 18,000 pieces of iron were
assembled in the tower's construction.

Above: The tower from the city.

Right: The city from the tower.

so inseparable from our image of Paris—was once destined to grace the streets of Barcelona. Eiffel originally presented the designs to the organizers of the 1888 Universal Exposition to be held there, but they were rejected, and the baton passed to Paris.

Construction of the Eiffel Tower involved a 300-strong workforce piecing together 18 thousand pieces of iron using two and a half million rivets. Given the perilous nature of the job and the size of the workforce, it would have been assumed that some lives would be lost, especially at a time when even a relatively small building project faced casualties. However, despite the lack of internal platforms, Eiffel ensured that every safety precaution was taken, and there was only one fatality on the three-year-long construction project.

As seems to be the way with artistic masterpieces when they are first created, the tower met with initial disapproval and was slated in many quarters. The opinion of the French novelist Guy de Maupassant was typical of many when he claimed that he ate his lunch daily in the tower's restaurant, purely so that he would not have to look at it—he did not want the sight of such an ugly monstrosity to ruin his lunch. A common complaint was about its perceived impracticality—many thought it would collapse at the first powerful gust of wind—but Eiffel was no amateur. He was an experienced engineer and insisted repeatedly that he had made precise mathematical calculations

in order to guarantee the tower's resilience. It certainly seems now, with hindsight, that he knew what he was doing. Another frequent objection was to the use of iron, which was deemed far too rough and ordinary for a national monument. Adverse feeling was so strong, in fact, that a group of artists formed a committee to campaign for the tower's destruction. They referred to the Eiffel Tower as a "gigantic black factory smokestack, crushing with its barbaric mass Notre Dame." An extract from their written petition illustrates the ferocity of the general antipathy towards the tower: "We come, writers, painters, sculptors, architects, passionate lovers of the beauty of Paris—a beauty until now unspoiled—to protest with all our might, in the name of slighted French taste, against the erection in the heart of our capital of the useless and monstrous Eiffel Tower. Are we going to allow all this beauty and tradition to be profaned? Is Paris now to be associated with the grotesque and mercantile imagination of a machine builder? To be defaced and disgraced? … We the committee are but a faint echo of universal sentiment, which is so legitimately outraged. When foreign visitors come to our universal exposition, they will cry out in astonishment 'What? Is this the atrocity that the French present to us as the representative of their vaunted national taste?' And they will be right to laugh at us."

Fortunately, their plea was unsuccessful, and twenty years later, when it was due to be torn down, public opinion

"Iron was deemed too rough and ordinary for a national monument."

Over: Providing an illuminated beacon at night.

Below: The Eiffel Tower in springtime.

had changed. The cry was now that it should be saved at all costs. Over the years, the Eiffel Tower has become inseparable from the name of Paris—one can hardly be thought of without thought of the other—to the extent that it is almost integral to national identity. Certainly, a uniquely French sense of humor emerges from various anecdotes attached to the tower. One involves a French con artist managing to pull off the apparent "sale" of the tower for scrap. Another details how during the Nazi occupation of Paris in 1940, the elevator cables were cut so that should Hitler wish to ascend the tower, he would have to climb the stairs. In the event, he sent his soldiers up to attach the Nazi flag to the top—but it promptly flew off in the wind, so they had to climb up again and fix another one in its place. Hitler himself remained firmly on the ground. As soon as the Nazis left Paris, the elevators were immediately back in full working order. As they were leaving, Hitler ordered the destruction of the tower, but the general who received the order did not carry it out because he did not want to be remembered as the man who had destroyed the Eiffel Tower. Fate seems to have conspired to save the Eiffel Tower against all the odds—the fact that it was never meant to stand for more than twenty years, the fact that it was widely disparaged when first built, even the fact that Hitler ordered its destruction but failed. Back in the 1920s, it was thought prudent to preserve the tower because of its usefulness in communications. Now, to do otherwise would simply be unthinkable.

Left: The romantic aura of tower and river illuminated at night.

Above: A full moon sits in one of the tower's elegant curves.

Over: The fine, detailed work of an artist-engineer.

"Fate seems to have conspired to save the Eiffel Tower against all the odds."

Right and Opposite: Mount Rushmore National Memorial, 60-foot-high sculptures representing 160 years of American history in South Dakota.

Over: The stony gazes of Washington, Jefferson, Roosevelt, and Lincoln in Mount Rushmore National Park.

Mount Rushmore

To date, Mount Rushmore is the largest work of art on Earth. It was designed to commemorate four giant figures from America's history, but its planning and construction were not without controversy.

Mount Rushmore Memorial Park is located near Keystone, South Dakota, within the United States Presidential Memorial. Carved from solid granite, the monument is representative of the first 150 years of the history of the United States of America through its depiction of four of its great presidents. Built at a cost of $989,992.32, it took fourteen years to complete, with the first rock carving beginning October 4, 1927, and ending on October 31, 1941.

Through the mountain's history, it has had many names before finally being recognized as Mount Rushmore. Rising to a height of 5,725 feet (1,745 m) above sea level, the mountain is the tallest in the region. The Lakota Sioux knew the mountain as Six Grandfathers. As white American settlers came into the area the peak was known as Cougar Mountain, Sugarloaf Mountain, Slaughterhouse Mountain, and the Keystone Cliffs. During a prospecting expedition in 1885, it was renamed Mount Rushmore, in honor of Charles E. Rushmore—a member of the expedition and prominent New York lawyer.

A proposal, made in 1923 by local historian Doane Robinson, to create the immense carving project as a way of increasing tourism in the Black Hills, found many supporters. However, for the local Lakota tribe, the project was very controversial from the start. In 1895, the Treaty of Fort Laramie had granted the Black Hills to the Lakota people. Yet, after the discovery of gold in the Black Hills was made public, the government made little effort to discourage prospecting on Native American land.

It had been Robinson's vision to see a giant memorial created to acknowledge great figures of the American West such as Buffalo Bill Cody, General George Armstrong Custer, Lewis and Clark, as well as historic Sioux warriors. Robinson persuaded sculptor Gutzon Borglum to travel to the Black Hills to decide if the massive sculpture was even feasible. Borglum, who had studied under French sculptor Auguste Rodin, had been working at Stone Mountain in Georgia on a large mountain bas-relief. The memorial was to commemorate Confederate leaders. As Borglum surveyed the Black Hills region, he discovered the Mount Rushmore cliff. Having chosen Mount Rushmore because it faced

Above: The benevolent face of Abraham Lincoln, carved into the granite of the Mount Rushmore and finished in September 1937.

Opposite and Over: Four great American presidents keep a watchful eye across the nation from the face of Mount Rushmore.

southeast—giving it maximum exposure to sunlight—he remarked, "America will march along that skyline." On March 3, 1925, Congress authorized the Mount Rushmore National Memorial Commission.

Though the final decision as to whose faces would be carved into the mountain fell to Borglum, it was President Coolidge who decided that the faces would be those of presidents of the United States. After the selection of George Washington, Coolidge (a Republican) decided the other figures should be two Republicans and a Democrat. The final line-up was

completed with the selection of Thomas Jefferson—who drafted the Declaration of Independence—Abraham Lincoln, and Theodore Roosevelt. Originally, the image of Thomas Jefferson was set to the right of Washington, but as the work on the Jefferson figure began, Borglum discovered that the rock in the area was unsuitable. Jefferson's image was moved to Washington's left side. Borglum's original carving design planed the figures to be depicted from head to waist.

From 1927, until its completion in 1941, nearly 400 local workers worked on the Mount Rushmore

Memorial. There were roads to be built, power to be generated, and pneumatic drill bits to be sharpened. Some workers used their expertise in setting dynamite charges, while others completed the more delicate finishing work on the faces of the giant sculpture. Using techniques Borglum had developed on his Stone Mountain project, his crews became so skilled at using dynamite that they could blast to within four inches of the finished surface and grade the contours of the lips, checks, nose, brow, and neck. They removed 450,000 tons of granite from the mountain, 90 percent of which was taken out by dynamiting. Amazingly, there were no deaths and very few injuries during the creation of the monument. Converting Borglum's model of the four presidents into the mountain was a feat in itself. The scale was 1:12, meaning that 1 inch (2.5 cm) on the model translated to 1 foot (30.5 cm) on the cliff. By mounting a protractor onto the head of the model, then using a similar apparatus on the cliff, workers were able to determine exactly how much rock needed to be removed. Using the same technique, drills were used to make closely-placed holes at exact depths. The rocks between the honeycombing of holes were broken away using chisels and hammers. A process known as "bumping," which used a pneumatic drill and a special bit, left the surface with a finish as smooth as a concrete sidewalk.

Nearing the completion of Mount Rushmore, Borglum feared that there would be no record of the creation of the monument. In 1938, a giant

vault was carved into the canyon wall behind Mount Rushmore. The Great Hall of Records—as it was to be known—was to house records of the memorial, of Western civilization, and of individual liberty and freedom. But Borglum never completed the project. Due to the U.S. involvement in World War II, and Borglum's sudden death, the project was left unfinished until 1998 when the National Park Service completed a scaled-down version of the hall. After the death of Borglum, his son, Lincoln, spent the next seven months refining final details on the monument. He stopped construction on Mount Rushmore on October 31, 1941 to leave the monument we know today.

To date, Rushmore is the largest work of art on the earth. Each face is 60 feet (18.2 m) high. By comparison, the head of the Statue of Liberty is only 17 feet (5.1 m) tall. The estimated erosion rate is only 1 inch (2.5 cm) every 10,000 years, thanks to the fine-grained granite composition of the mountain. Mount Rushmore is still a controversial subject among Native Americans, even after the appointment as superintendent of the park of the first Native American, Gerard Baker, in 2004. As a response to the Mount Rushmore memorial, the Crazy Horse Memorial is under construction in the Black Hills to commemorate the famous Native American leader. When completed, the memorial will be larger than Mount Rushmore. The Crazy Horse Memorial has the support of the Lakota chiefs, and to date, the Crazy Horse Memorial Foundation has rejected all offers of federal funding.

Panama Canal

The Panama Canal, a huge marvel of engineering, consists of seventeen artificial lakes, several improved and artificial channels, and two sets of locks. It completely transformed shipping and travel between the Atlantic and Pacific Oceans, reducing the time and distance needed to voyage between the two.

Right: A few of the 14,000 vessels per year to traverse the Panama Canal.

Opposite: A ship passes through the Gatun Locks, one of two vast locks on Panama Canal.

One of the largest and most difficult engineering feats ever undertaken, the Panama Canal is a ship canal just over 50 miles (82 km) long, which bisects the isthmus of the Central American country of Panama. Connecting the Caribbean Sea with the Pacific Ocean, it is one of the most important shipping routes in the world.

The canal is also one of the most spectacular sights in the already beautiful country of Panama, with its vast locks filling with water to allow grand ships to pass between the steep lush green mountains.

Take, for example, the Gatun locks at the Atlantic entrance to this wonderful canal, the largest along its structure.

As you watch, great ships hover into view, slowly lining up, one by one. Then each vessel slides through three sets of locks, where each one is closed and filled to raise the ship up inch by inch, until the ship finally glides out onto the waters of Lake Chagres.

Rather than being a straight waterway like many other canals in the world,

however, the Panama Canal consists of seventeen artificial lakes, several improved and artificial channels, and two sets of locks. An additional artificial lake, Alajuela Lake, acts as a reservoir for the canal to ensure its water levels are always high enough for the locks to function and to ease each ship's passage.

Opened on August 15, 1914, the project was begun by the French in 1881. When they abandoned it in 1889, the United States took over and won the construction rights after Panama declared its independence in 1903.

However, neither the French nor the Americans were the first to come up with the idea of trying to curtail the tortuous sea voyage around the southern tip of South America and Cape Horn. A ship sailing from New York to San Francisco via the canal travels 6,000 miles (9,500 km), well under half the distance of the previous 14,000 miles (22,500 km) route around Cape Horn.

The earliest proposition for a man-made waterway cutting across the Central American isthmus—or narrow land bridge—dates back to 1534, when King Charles V of Spain suggested that a canal would ease the voyage for ships traveling to and from Ecuador and Peru. However, wars in Europe put the project on permanent hold.

Over the following centuries, other ways of navigating the narrow land between the two oceans were attempted. In 1698, the Kingdom of Scotland launched the ill-fated Darien scheme to set up an overland trade route, but they had underestimated the inhospitable conditions of the rainforests and abandoned the idea in 1700.

In 1819, the Spanish government revived the idea of a canal and formally authorized the construction of the waterway. Various surveys were done between 1850 and 1875, and these showed that only two routes were practical—one across Panama and another across Nicaragua.

Nothing happened with the canal, but the Panama Railway was built across the isthmus and finally opened in 1855. Ironically, this overland transport link was a massive boost for trade across the land and became a key factor in the selection of the later canal route.

Galvanized by this and the success of the Suez Canal, an international company was formed in 1876 to build the canal. Two years later, it obtained agreement to dig the structure across the isthmus. However, the company collapsed, and in 1880, a French company led by Ferdinand Marie de Lesseps—the builder of the Suez Canal—began work on the Panamanian canal.

However, the workers suffered from disease, lack of experience with complex mountain ranges, and a high death toll—caused by malaria, yellow fever, and landslides. They also had to contend with the vicious humidity and ferociously high jungle temperatures. Although no detailed official records were maintained, it is thought that as many as 22,000 workers died before

Left: 40 vessels a day traverse the Panama Canal.

Over: Tourists view the passage of a vast container ship known as a Panamax—the largest vessels able to use to canal at present.

the French finally called a halt to construction in 1889.

A few years later, sensing an opportunity, President Theodore Roosevelt ordered the buyout of the French equipment. After helping Panama gain independence from Colombia—in exchange for control of the Panama Canal Zone— the Americans began work on the canal in 1904.

The US authorities then set to work and spent a considerable amount of money trying to eradicate some of the diseases from the region, particularly yellow fever and malaria. Once the spread of these infectious illnesses was under control, and after

significant work on the infrastructure, construction began. Ten years later, on August 15, 1914, the Panama Canal opened. The first ship to use the new canal was the Ancon, a cement boat that had been used in the construction of the canal.

But despite the advances in medicine during this period—including the discovery of the causes of yellow fever and malaria—5,609 workers died during these ten years of construction. But, the total death toll—combining all the attempts at construction—was around 27,500, or 550 souls for every mile of the canal's length.

Construction on the canal continues to this day. Even as far back as the

1930s, worries were raised that the water supply to the canal—needed to keep its locks filled—could prove to be a problem. As a result, the Madden Dam was constructed across the Chagres River. Completed in 1935, the dam created Lake Alajuela, which provides additional water for the canal.

After World War II, U.S. control of the canal, and the Canal Zone surrounding it, became controversial, particularly as relations between the two countries worsened.

Many Panamanians felt that the Canal Zone belonged to Panama. Negotiations between the U.S. and Panama began in 1974 and resulted in the Torrijos-Carter Treaty. Signed by President Jimmy Carter and General Omar Torrijos, president of Panama, on September 7, 1977, the treaty established that ownership of the canal should be ceded to Panama. Despite the treaty having been controversial in the U.S., Panama took control of the canal on December 31, 1999.

There were fears that efficiency and maintenance would suffer after the handover, however, these fears appear to have been unfounded.

The Panamanians are still looking to the future too. An enlargement scheme to allow more, and larger, ships to pass through the canal had been under consideration for many years. The proposal, which is expected to cost around $5.25 billion, was finally approved by national referendum on October 22, 2006.

Below: Luxurious cruise liners regularly use the canal to travel from the Caribbean to the Pacific Ocean.

Inset opposite: The Panamanian flag flies proudly from one of the canal's administrative buildings.

Left: Construction on the canal continues to this day.

Over: Limon Bay, or Bahia Limon, on the Atlantic coast of Panama, where ships can moor awaiting transit across the canal near the city of Cristobal.

Even now, before expansion, about 40 vessels a day traverse the canal. Every ship must pay to use the canal, and the fees, which are decided by the Panama Canal Authority, are based on vessel type, size, and the type of cargo that the vessel is carrying. The most expensive toll levied to date was $249,165, which was charged to the container ship Maersk Dellys on May 30, 2006. The least expensive toll was 36 cents charged to Richard Halliburton, an American adventurer, who swam the canal in 1928. The average toll, however, is around $54,000.

In light of the cost of tolls, it is worth bearing in mind that construction costs for the canal reached $375 million. This includes the $10 million paid to Panama and $40 million paid to the French company for the rights to the canal—not to mention the human cost expended for what is still, without a doubt, one of the architectural wonders of the world.

Houses of Parliament, London

The Palace of Westminster, also known as the Houses of Parliament, contains a labyrinth of rooms and corridors that the newcomer would find impossible to negotiate. The British House of Commons and House of Lords perform their legislative duties within its grand surroundings.

The building in which the two houses of the British parliament meet—the House of Lords and the House of Commons—is properly called the Palace of Westminster. But the parliamentary function has become so much a part of its very fabric that the building itself is often referred to as the Houses of Parliament. It is situated in the London Borough of Westminster, on the north bank of the River Thames, and the presence of parliament has taken over the borough to such an extent that events in politics generally are referred to as "events in Westminster."

The existing building is relatively recent, dating only from 1834, when it was rebuilt after a devastating fire had reduced it to rubble. However, a royal palace has stood on this land since Saxon times, and the existing Westminster Hall, within the building, dates back to 1097. Westminster Palace as it stands today is the work of architects Sir Charles Barry and Augustus Pugin, and it was built in the Gothic style.

Right: A viewfinder picks out the Houses of Parliament and Big Ben.

Left: Close-up of the clock tower which houses the "Big Ben" bell.

In medieval times, the area was known as Thorney Island and it was outside the City of London. When Edward the Confessor, one of the last Saxon kings, built an abbey to function as a Benedictine monastery in the 11th century, the area became known as West Monastery, which eventually became Westminster (hence Westminster Abbey). It was not until the reign of Edward I, late in the 13th century, that the idea of a "parliament" was first established, but subsequent British parliaments have met within these walls ever since the first official gathering of 1295.

After fire destroyed the palace in 1834, during the reign of Queen Victoria, there was much debate as to the style in which it should be rebuilt. Neoclassical (the style popularized by the White House) was considered, but politically it had associations with republicanism, which was deemed an inappropriate "statement" for a monarchy. Sir Charles Barry's designs in the Gothic Perpendicular style eventually emerged victorious from the arduous competition. Westminster

DOMINE : SALVAM : FAC : REGINAM : NOSTRAM : VICTORIAM : PRIMAM

Abbey had been built in the Gothic style, which first came to England from France in the 13th century. It underwent a revival in popularity during the 19th century, and so the style of the Palace of Westminster is known as Gothic Revival, whereas Westminster Abbey is simply Gothic. Sir Charles Barry was in fact a Classicist, but he was aided in his work by the Gothic architect Augustus Pugin, who disapproved of much of the "Greek" ordered symmetry in Barry's designs. The Gothic style was at the time considered to be conservative, but it has since become affiliated with the world of fantasy, and certainly the spiky peaks, pointed arches, and sharp jutting towers—typical of the Gothic style—lend the palace the look of a quaintly-turreted fairytale castle, rather than a place where serious business is conducted.

The palace was rebuilt in sand-colored limestone, but its quality was not sufficiently durable, and over the years in has had to be extensively restored and replaced, a process that continues to this day. The most striking feature of the building from afar is its towers. The Union Jack flies from the Victoria Tower, which houses the entrance used by the monarch (the flag is changed to the Royal Standard if the monarch is within the building). St. Stephen's Tower, the only one with a spire, is octagonal, and its original function was to bring high-level air into the palace. Now it houses the entrance by which Members of Parliament enter the Commons. But the most famous of all the towers is the one often erroneously referred to as Big Ben. The elegant, ornately carved clock tower is one of London's chief landmarks, and it is popularly known as Big Ben, although that name really applies to the largest of the five bells within the tower that chime the quarter hours. "Big Ben" is actually a nickname for the Great Bell of Westminster.

The Palace of Westminster is a labyrinth of endless rooms and corridors that the newcomer would find impossible to negotiate. There are over 1,000 rooms, 100 staircases, and 3.1 miles (5 km) of hallways. The most notable rooms are the chambers in which the House of Lords and the House of Commons sit. The Lords' chamber is decorated predominantly in red, and it boasts fine artistic features such as the stained glass windows representing law, chivalry, and religion. It also contains the gold throne on which the Queen sits at the annual ceremony called the State Opening of Parliament. A quaint feature of the viewing gallery is a low-level curtain, installed in the 1920s, which was designed to hide the ankles and legs of viewing ladies and thus protect the delicate Lords' modesty. The Commons' chamber is predominantly green and far less ornate. Perhaps the most intriguing details in its decoration are two red lines on the floor, one on each side of the chamber. No speaker from any political party is meant to cross the red line on his side. Legend has it that they are spaced exactly two swords' lengths and a foot apart in order to prevent disagreements from turning into duels.

"The name Big Ben really applies to the largest of the five bells within the tower."

Left: Golden ornamentation on the clock's face.

The oldest part of the building, dating back to 1097, is Westminster Hall. The hall was originally the Royal Court, which saw such important trials as that of King Charles I after the English Civil War. It later hosted coronation banquets and lyings-in-state for the funerals of the great and mighty, including Sir Winston Churchill. Its most outstanding feature is the oak hammerbeam, or open timber, roof. Spanning over 68 feet (21 m) across and 239 feet (73 m) in length, it is the largest unsupported roof in Europe.

Before the fire that destroyed the original palace, there was another notorious attempt at its destruction. The Gunpowder Plot of 1605 was the work of Catholic noblemen who wanted to annihilate the Protestant monarchy represented by King James I. They planted explosives underneath the palace—the plan being to detonate them at the State Opening of Parliament, killing the king, his family, and most of the aristocracy. The plot was uncovered when a Roman Catholic Lord was given prior warning not to attend the ceremony, and the explosives were discovered, along with one plotter whose name has gone down in British history—Guy Fawkes.

Fawkes and his fellow conspirators were arrested and tried for treason. They were found guilty and executed. Fawkes' failed attempt to destroy Westminster Palace is still commemorated in Britain every year on November 5, when people light bonfires and set off fireworks. To some,

Above: The Palace of Westminster illuminated at night seen across the River Thames.

Opposite: Intricate "Gothic" details in the stonework.

Over: Some of the Palace's one thousand plus rooms.

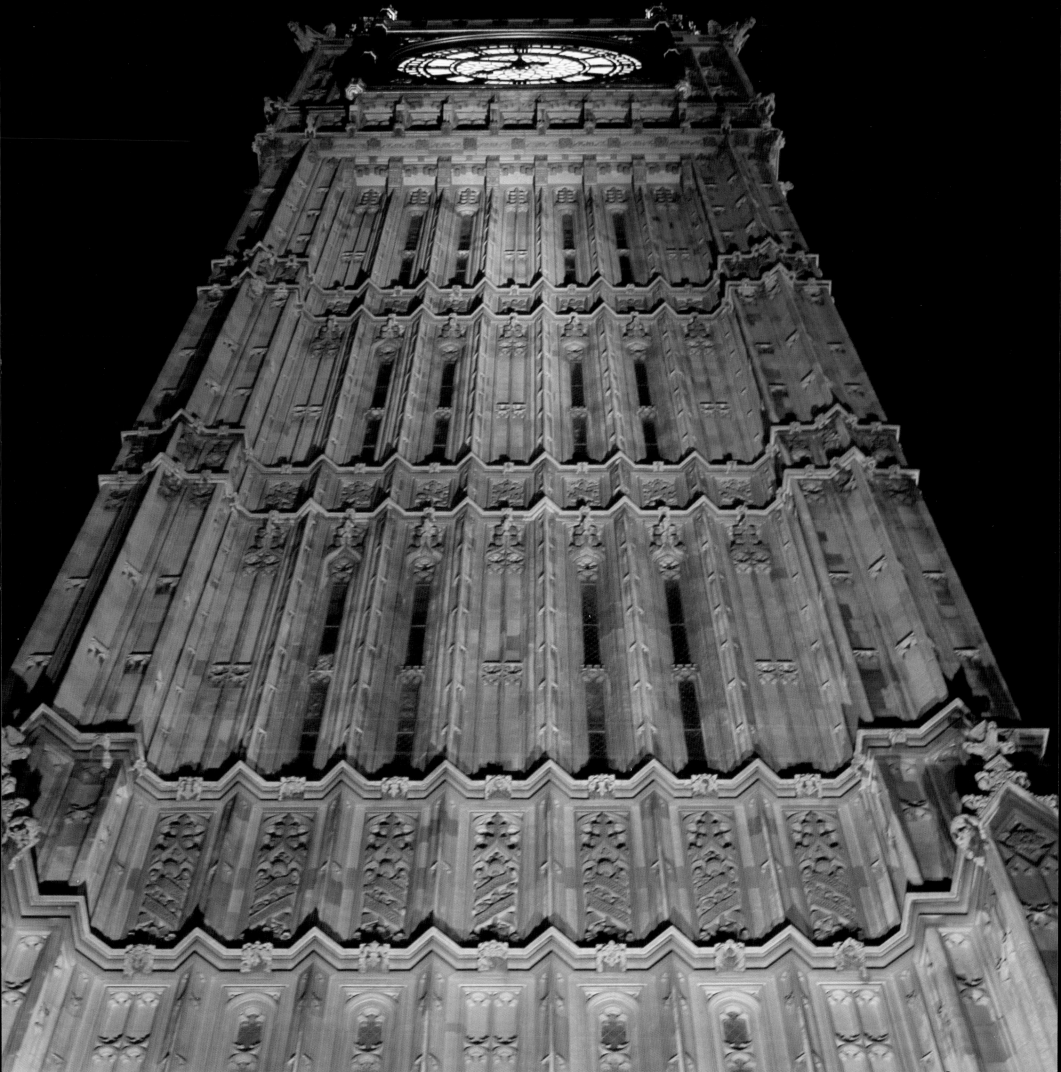

Above: A red double-decker bus passes Big Ben.

Right: The pointed features characteristic of Gothic architecture.

the celebration honors the fact that the plot was foiled, but other people celebrate the attempt that was made to destroy this seat of power and authority!

As might be expected of an official building with such a long and colorful history, there are many long-standing traditions associated with the Palace of Westminster. Every year at the ceremony for the State Opening of Parliament, which marks the start of the annual Parliamentary session, Queen Elizabeth II dons her crown and other regalia and then travels the short distance from her home in Buckingham Palace to the Houses of Parliament in a horse-drawn golden carriage. Before the Queen can enter to deliver her official speech to the assembled members of Parliament, the Yeomen of the Guard traditionally conduct a "search" of the cellars of the building to ensure that no one is planning another Gunpowder Plot. No monarch or other member of the Royal Family is permitted to set foot inside the House of Commons, so a representative of the Queen—called "Black Rod" because of the ceremonial staff he carries—is sent to summon the members of the House of Commons to come and listen to the Queen's speech. As Black Rod approaches the door to the House of Commons, it is ceremonially slammed in his face, to symbolize the House of Commons' independence from the monarch. Black Rod then uses his staff to knock three times on the door to alert the members that their presence is required. But just as the sovereign is not permitted to enter the House of Commons, the

members of the House of Commons are not officially permitted inside the House of Lords because the latter is the exclusive domain of the nobility. Thus the elected members must remain standing and crowd around the outside of the chamber to listen as the Queen outlines the legislative policy for the coming year.

The chamber of the House of Commons was severely damaged in an air bombing attack during World War II. After the war was over, the chamber was rebuilt. Care was taken to ensure that the original architectural features of the chamber were retained. Reconstruction was completed in 1950.

It is possible for members of the public to gain admission to observe parliamentary debates in the House of Commons and the House of Lords. Anyone who has seen television coverage of the debates in the House of Commons will know that the exchanges can become very heated. The layout of the chamber contributes to the adversarial atmosphere, with the rows of green-upholstered benches arranged in two facing sets along the long sides of the chamber. This is very different from the semicircular arrangement featured in parliamentary chambers of many other countries around the world.

Such lively debates are part and parcel of the long tradition of democracy and legislative authority that the Houses of Parliament have witnessed through the years.

Above: Night vista over the Thames

Over: The seat of government sits majestic on its river bank.

"No monarch is permitted to set foot inside the House of Commons."

Useful Information

General

http://www.new7wonders.com
An international election which allows the public to vote on a new version of the tradition Seven Wonders of the World. The day of judgment is 07/07/07.

http://www.unesco.org
World Heritage website: its mission "to encourage the identification, protection, and preservation of cultural and natural heritage around the world."

Buildings

http://www.goldengatebridge.org
The official website, providing current information and history.

http://www.nps.gov
National Parks Service. Interesting in relation to parkland around the bridge.

http://www.cntower.ca/
The official website providing current information, images and history.

http://www.greatbuildings.com/ buildings/Gateway_Arch.html
A very informative site, which also has information on several other architectural treats.

http://www.copacabana.info/ christ-the-redeemer.html
Includes history, pictures and interesting information on the Statue.

http://www.pancanal.com/
The official website, providing current information and history on the Panama Canal.

http://www.usbr.gov/lc/ hooverdam/History/storymain.html
Offers a very full description on the history of the dam, as well as current information on tours.

http://mountrushmore.areaparks. com/
A useful website for general information about Mount Rushmore.

http://www.londoneye.com/ AboutEye.aspx
The official website providing current information, images and history.

http://www.tour-eiffel.fr
The official website of the Eiffel Tower.

http://www.paris.org/monuments
Further information regarding the Eiffel Tower.

http://www.grandcentralterminal. com
The official website, providing current information and history.

http://www.petronastwintowers. com
The official website of the Petronas Twin Towers.

http://www.statueofliberty.org/
Provides several interesting facts on the Statue of Liberty and Ellis Island, including a free passenger records search.

http://www.parliament.uk
Everything you need to know about the British government, its workings, its history and its buildings.

http://www.esbnyc.com/index2. cfm
The official website of the Empire State Building.

http://www.sydneyharbourbridge. info/
An informative, detailed website on the Sydney Harbor Bridge.

http://www.sydneyoperahouse. com/
The official website of the Sydney Opera House.

Index